Encyclopaedia of Child Labour

Encyclopaedia of Child Labour

Volume-1

Status of Child Labour

Promila Mahajan
S. Chand

Adhyayan Publishers & Distributors
Delhi-110094

Published by
ADHYAYAN PUBLISHERS & DISTRIBUTORS
L-9 B, Street No. 42, Sadatpur Extension
Delhi-110094
Ph.: 011-22191282, Fax : 011-22199182
E-mail : adhyayanpublishers@yahoo.com

Encyclopaedia of Child Labour
(2 Vols.)

Ist Edition : 2006
ISBN - 81-89161-77-6 (Set)

Printed in India

Published by Harish Chandra Yadav for Adhyayan Publishers & Distributors, Laser Typesetting at Himanshu Printers and Printed at Tarun Offset Printers, Delhi.

Preface

The future of any nation depends upon the sound development of children. As Wordsworth has also said 'Child is the Father of Man'. For construction of civilized, cultural and happy society, we have to educate and train our children properly because tomorrow they would take the nation towards prosperity. The ilimenation of child labour and their rehabilitation has emerged as an important area of scientific work. It has been seen that a large number of child labour are surviving under great health and safety hazards. Above all the workplace trauma is widespread, stunting the growth of the child both physically and mentally.

Hence, considering the problem in its totality, an effort has been made to cover the diverse aspects of the subject. All the articles are judiciously selected from authoritative sources. We are grateful to all the learned authors and academicians whose writings are cited or substantially made use of in these volumes. This Encyclopaedia has been divided into two volumes in which each volume is complete in it self.

They are as follows:

1. Status of Child Labour
2. Case Studies and Legal Interventions

This joint effort has been taken as an academic exercise to provide an over all view on issues and problems related to child labour at macro, meso and micro level, including the valuable contributions from social scientists, planners and administrators to present a more comprehensive view on the subject.

Students, teachers, researchers, administrators, policy planners and professionals from different streams of disciplines would find this Encyclopaedia informative and useful.

The Editors are also very grateful to Shri Harish Chandra Yadav of Adhyayan Publishers & Distributors, Delhi for taking keen interest in publishing it in very short time.

Promila Mahajan

S. Chand

Editors

Contents

1

Child Labour : An Introduction

The significance and the importance of the child lies in the fact that the child is universe. If there was no child, there would be no humanity and there can not be a universe without humanity. Therefore, mankind owes to the child the best that it has to be given. 1 If there is no proper growth of child today. The future of the country will be in dark. It is thus an obligation of every generation to bring up children who will be citizen of tomorrow in a proper way. Today's children will be the leader who will hold the country s banner high and maintain the prestige of the nation. If a child goes wrong for want of proper attention, training and guidance, it will indeed be a deficiency of the society and of government of the day. Every society must, therefore, devote full attention to ensure that children are properly cared for and brought up in a proper atmosphere where they would receive adequate training, education and guidance in order that they may be able to have their rightful place in society when they grew up.

Both at the national level and the international level great interest is being shown in the matter of welfare of children. Children need special protection because of their tender age, physique and mental facilities. They are a "supremely important national asset," and the future well being of the nation depends as to how children grow and develop. They need special law to protect them from exploitation and fraud, to save them from certain liabilities and to develop their personality in view of them weak position. A study team of social welfare has rightly stated: "The importance of child welfare services lies in the consideration that the personality of man is built up in the formative years, and the physical and mental health of the nation is determined largely by the manner in which it is shaped in the early stages."

It is not an exaggeration to say that the children are the blooming flowers of the garden of society and so, it is our duty to protect these flowers from damaging effects of excessive exposure to heat, cold and rain. It is quite imperative to give vent to the thought of Hon'ble Mr. Justice Suba Rao who has rightly observed: "Social justice must begin with children. Unless tender plant is properly tendered and nourished, it has little chance to growing into a strong and useful tree. So, first priority in the scale of social justice shall be given to the welfare of children. Similarly, Gabrial, Mistral of Chile, Nobal prize winning poet, has rightly highlighted:

"We are guilty of many faults, but our worst crime is abandoning the children, neglecting the fountain of life. Many of the things we need can wait. The child cannot. Right now is the time his bones are being formed, his blood is being made and his sense being developed. To him, we can not answer, 'Tomorrow.' His name is 'Today.'

Today there are no two opinions that the children are the hope of parents and future of the nation and thus be given adequate opportunities and facilities for developing themselves.

The growth of the child into a mature and happy person with fully developed personality largely depends upon the support and attention he receives from the society. If a child does not get proper education, diet and other facilities, his very development into a self sustaining human being is dwarfed, The child because of his physical and mental inmaturity needs special safeguards, it becomes, therefore, the duty of state to protect children's right by legislative and other means. The needs and requirements of the child, the primordial ground norm of this universe. the most innocent and helpless human being incapable of enforcing his legal rights, but to speak of demanding new rights obligate the state to secure him distributive justice. As distinguished from adults, children are peculiarly susceptible to certain harms. They cannot raise their voice against those who injure them or deprive them of their rights. The peculiar position of the child arising from his physical and mental disability and position of dependence recognizes the need for the special provisions in many matters and the law should take care of all this in the interest and general welfare of child. The protective arm of the law has, therefore, to be long and strong enough if distributive justice to the adults of tomorrow is to be secured.

However, the reality lies in the fact that child still has not been given proper attention and is being exploited by the people who achieve their selfish ends. This is quite evident from the Report of Director-General of International Labour Organization published in 1960, though the acute estimate of child labour, either from a qualitative or quantitative point of view, is not possible, yet the report discloses that:

"Children and youth make up a fifth to a fourth or even a third of the total labour forces in many of the industrializing countries. Young people (between) 15 to 19 make up 20 percent of the labour force of the Egyptian Region of the United Arab Republic, and a higher percentage in many of less developed Asian and African countries, and it should be noted that in most of the less developed areas the great bulk of children seek to enter the labour force by the time they are 12,13 or 14, if they have not begun to work at a much earlier age."

It is estimated that by 2000 A.D. 25 per cent of the world's population will be children and 40 per cent of the entire global labour force will be below the age of 15 years. In developing countries 40 per cent of the total population under 15 years and 75 per cent are employed as child labour. International Labour Organization in a study concluded that in Asian Countries 70 to 80 per cent of children are either working or "simply wasting their lives away." Employment of children has continued therefore to be a problem.

Nature of the Problem

Child labour is not a new phenomenon to our age. What is new, however, is its perception as a social problem the world over. There has been a distinct change in recent past in the values and attitudes of the legitimizing groups of society vis-a-vis child labour because of some new developments. In the pre-industrial agricultural society of India, children worked as helpers and learners in hereditarily determined family occupations under the benign supervision of adult family members. The work place was an extension of the home and work was characterized by personal informal relationships. The tasks and technology that work involved were simple and non-hazardous which the child could learn smoothly, almost unconsciously, over the years through association and limitation.

The social scenario, however, changed radically with the advent of industrialization and urbanization under the impact of the newly generated centrifugal and centripetal forces, there was an unbroken stream of the rural poor migrating to urban centers in search of livelihood. The child had to work as an individual person either under an employer or independently. His work environment endangered his physical health and mental growth and led to his exploitation. The protection and welfare of these children, therefore, become an issue of paramount social significance.

Another sociological factor bearing on the problem of child labour was the emergence of welfare consciousness on a world scale. The industrial revolution in the west generated such vast demands for manpower that even children had to be pressed into service. Contemporary writings reveals under what atrocious conditions. These children had to work in coal mines and textile mills. However, once the West had built up its affluence and the baneful effects of child labour become out rageously manifest, the state took appropriate measures to meet the evil. The welfare measures enunciated had a universal appeal to human conscience. In the more recent past they have been thoughtfully embodied in various resolutions of the ILO and other organs of the United nations. Countries of the less developed world, after their emancipation from colonial domination, also accepted a number of these resolutions even though their social and economic infrastructure was still inadequate for fulfilling all the commitments. Free India has similarly embodied in its constitution many

provisions establishing thereby the normative superiority of welfare considerations over the economic one and has endeavored to weed out the antagonism between child labour and child development.

Yet another factor highlighting the evil aspect of child labour is the recent advances in various sciences having a bearing on the child. Today, scientific knowledge has revolutionized our outlook on the care of child and his developmental imperatives. Diffusion on this knowledge has created a new awareness in the major institutions of society as to the relationship the child should have with his milieu, his need objects and his work, etc.

Child labour, of late, has evoked deep concern. However, we must make a distinction between child labour and exploitation of child labour. Both are a problem though of different orders. Child labour as distinguished from work experience has mostly negative attributes. It can now be asserted on scientific grounds that work as a direct fulfillment of the child's natural abilities and creative potentialities is always conducive to his healthy growth. But work when taken up as a means for the fulfillment of some other needs becomes enslaving in character and deleterious in its impact. Labour is work of the latter type irrespective of the degree of strain or exploitation involved in it. Labour in the case of child is especially harmful because the energy that should have been expanded on the nutriting of his latent powers is consumed for purposes of base survival.

Child labour is as much the cause as consequence of adult unemployment and under-employment. It at once supplements and depresses the family income. Child labour is not only a subsidy to industry but a direct inducement to the payment to low wages to adult workers. The entrance of the children into the labour market reduces the volume of employment for the adult and lowers he bargaining power of adult workers. Regions of childhood employment result in a permanently weakened and damaged labour force. Child labour involves the use of labour as its point of lowest productivity. Hence, it is an inefficient utilization of labour power. The argument that employment of children. increases the earnings of the family and keeps children away from mischief is misleading. It glasses over the fact that child labour deprives children of educational opportunities minimizes their chances for vocational training, stunts their physical growth, hampers their intellectual development and, by forcing them into the army of unskilled labourers or blind alley jobs, condemns them to low wages all their lives.

Compelled by the exigencies of situations children accept role which run them into both victims and involuntary accomplices of unjust situations. In many situation which is characterized by the fact that if one does not work. One has the option of either starving or adopting socially disapproved means for one's survival, children have no choice but to decide to take up jobs at an age at which they should have gone to school. Though at the fact, of it, it appears that it is the children who take the decision to work but the fact remain that it is not the children but the society to which they belong which though its inability to provide adequate means of subsistence for their families decides at the time of their conception itself that they are destined to be forced to take up employment at an early age. Mendelievich has rightly maintained: "It is not the family that should carry the blame for the fact that the child has to work, since the courses of action open to the family are few in number. It is society as a whole that is at fault. It is not only the children who are harmed due to their involvement in various kind of work at the tender age but the society also which has to suffer a great loss because of children being employed by employer who always make their best efforts to export minimum benefits with minimum investment. The employment of children adversely affects not only the employment opportunities of others forcing many to remain jobless in the present age but also considerably lowers the rates of their wages. In fact, it has been rightly maintained in the Report of Committee on Child Labour "Child Labour is as much as the cause as consequence of adult unemployment and under employment. It at once supplements and depresses the family income." Mendelievich has correctly depicted the picture of various circles that exists between child labour and poverty in the society. There is in fact a vicious circle here on the one hand, child labour increases unemployment among adults and reduces their income, on the other, the unemployment and low wages of adults force them to put their children to work in order to boost the family income. Thus child labour simultaneously increases and reduces the family income; but as is clear, it reduces rather than increases that income.

MEANING OF CHILD LABOUR

A generally valid definition of child labour is presently

not available either in the national or international context. Any definition turns upon the precise meaning we attach to two components of the term "child labour." i.e., "child" in terms of his chronological age, and "labour" in terms of its nature, quantum and income generation capacity. Child labour, however, can broadly be defined as that segment of the child population which participates in work either paid or unpaid.

The definition of child labour varied from one act to another depending upon the seriousness of the problems of children working in a particular employment. The precise age of what constitute child labour has not been laid down anywhere because of variations in the age of child as given under different legislative enactments. Section 82 of the Indian Penal Code reads: "Nothing is an offense which is done by a child under 7 years of age. Section 83 of the Indian Penal code, 1860, provides, "Nothing is an offense which is done by a child above 7 years and under 12 who has not attained sufficient maturity of understanding to judge the nature and consequence of his conduct on the occasion. Section 105 of Indian Evidence Act, 1872, lays down, "When a person is accused of any offense, the burden of proving the existence of circumstances bringing the case within any of the general or special exception including that of childhood of the Indian Penal Code or any concerning law is upon him."

Under the Indian majority Act, 1874 the age of majority has been fixed at 18 years. Under the Vaccination Act, 1880, children have been defined as person, "who have not attained the age of 14 years in case of boys and 18 years in case of girls." Under the Reformatory School Act, 1887."Youth Offender" means any boy who has been convicted of any offense punishable with imprisonment for life or death and who at the time of such conviction, was under the age of 15 years. "The Child Marriage Restraint Act, 1929 (Sharda Act) defines child as "a male below twenty-one years and a female below eighteen years of age.

According to Employment of children Act, 1938, "No child

who has not completed his fifteen years shall be employed or permitted to work in any occupation ... No child who has completed his fifteen years but has not completed his seventeenth year shall be employed or permitted to work in any occupation unless the period of work of such child for any day are so fixed as to allow an interval of rest for at least twelve consecutive hours which shall include at least seven consecutive hours between 10 P.M. and 7 A.M. as may be prescribed ...No child who has not completed his fourteenth year shall be employed or permitted to work in any workshop within any of the processes set forth in the schedule is carried on.

Under the Motor Vehicles Act, 1939, child has been defined as a person under the age of 18 years. According to the U.P.Children Act, 1951,"child" means a person under the age of 16 years. As per the plantation of Labour Act,1951 "child" means a person who has not completed his fifteenth year." Section 24 of the Act lays down: "No child who has not completed his twelfth year shall be required or allowed to work in any plantation. The young person as or a person under the age of 20 years. Under the Suppression of Immoral Traffic in Women and Girls Act, 1956,"girl" means a female who has not completed the age of 21 years." According to the Orphanages and Charitable Homes (Supervision and Control) Act, 1960. "child" means a boy or girl who has not completed the age of eighteen years. As per the provisions of the Children Act,1960. "child" means a boy who has attained the age of 18 years.

In the Merchant Shipping Act,1958, employment of children below fifteen years as seamen has ordinarily been prohibited. Persons below eighteen years cannot be employed as trimmer and stokers. According to the Motor Transport Worker's Act, 1961,"child" means a person who has not completed his fifteen years. Section 21 of the Act provides: "No child shall be required or allowed to work in any capacity in any motor transport undertaking." Section 22 lays down: "No adolescent shall be required or allowed to work as a motor transport worker in any motor transport undertaking unless-

(a) a certificate of fitness granted with reference to him ...is in the custody of the employer, and(b) such adolescent carries with him while he is at work, a token giving a reference to such certificate." "Adolescent." according to Section 2 (a) of the Act, "means a person who has completed his fifteenth year but has not completed his eighteenth year.'

Under the Radiation Protection Rules, 1971, farmed under the Atomic Energy Act, 1962, "A child has been defined as a person below eighteen years of age." According to Section 2(2) of the U.P.Dookan Aur Vanijya Adhishthan Adhiniyam, 1962, "child" means a person who has not completed his fourteenth year." Section 1 of the Act clearly says: "No child shall be required or allowed to work in any shop or commercial establishment except as an apprentice in such employment as may be notified by the state government in the gazette.

In shops and Commercial Establishment Acts passed by other states and union territories, child has been defined as a person between 12 and 14 years. It is because of this variation in age of child in different laws but the child labour will have to be defined in the context of a vocation in which a child is employed. According to Section 2(b) of the Bidi and Cigar Workers (Conditions of Employment) Act 1966. "child" means a person who has not completed fourteenth year of age." Section 24 of the Act provides, "No child shall be required or allowed to work in any industrial premises."

The work 'child labour' has been differently defined in various studies. According to the committee on child labour, "child labour, however, can broadly be defined as that segment of child population in work either paid or unpaid." In their study of working children in Bombay, Singh, and others have held a view: "child labour means a working child who is between 6 and 15 years of age," is not attending school during the day, is working under an employer or is learning some trade as an apprentice. "In the study titled as working children as working children in urban Delhi conducted by the Indian Council of

Child Welfare. "Every child below 14 years, who contributed to the family income or was gainfully employed including those marginally working was treated as a worker."

Sri V.V. Giri has expressed the view: The term "child labour is commonly interrupted in two different ways: first, as an economic practice and second, as a social evil. In the first context it signifies employment of children in gainful occupations with a view to adding to the total income of the family. It is in the second sense that the term child labour is now more generally used. In assessing the nature and extent of social evil, it is necessary to take into account the character of the jobs on which children are engaged, the danger to which they are exposed and the opportunities of development of which they have been denied.

Hommerfolks, Chairman of the United Nation Child Labour Committee, has defined child labour as or any work by children that interferes with their full physical development, their opportunities for a desirable level of education of their needed recreation. Kulshreshtha is of the view that, child labour in a restricted sense means the employment of child in gainful occupations which are dangerous to their health and deny them the opportunities of development ... The term child labour not only applies to the children working in the industries but also to the children in all forms of nonindustrial occupations which are injurious to their physical, mental, moral and social development." According to Alakh Narayan Sharma," child labour means the employment of children in gainful occupations (in industrial as well as non-industrial occupations) which are injurious to their physical, mental moral and social development. Thus, the term includes wage-labour as well as self-employed children working independently as well as in family enterprises. Child labour therefore, can be defined here as any work undertaken by children below 14 years in such works which are injurious to their health, and harmful to their proper development.

MAGNITUDE OF THE PROBLEM OF CHILD LABOUR

The problem of child labour in India is also of immense magnitude when one considers the number of children involved. According to the 1971 census, there were 10.74 million children working, representing 4.66 percent of total population and 5.95 percent of the total labour force. According to the 1981 census, workers in the age group below 14 years of age (excluding Assam) were 13.59 million. On the basis of the National Sample survey (32nd Round) the number of child workers as on 1st March, 1983 was 17.36 million. The working children mainly belong to the age group 5-14 years. Nearly 93 percent of the total child labour force works in the rural areas and the rest in urban areas. A great majority of these children work in agriculture and the unorganized sector like small commercial establishments and shops or quasi family undertakings. 79 percent are employed as cultivators or agricultural labourers, 8 percent in livestock, forestry, plantations,etc., 6 per cent in household and other services, the rest in trade, commerce and transport. Various surveys conducted by the labour bureau reveal that children are employed to do light job, such as helping in the field , in factories for packing, pasting of labels, etc. and in match factories, tea factories, tea estates, bidi manufacturing, printing, publishing, etc. Unorganized sector employs a large number of children as domestic servants, works in hotels, restaurants, canteens, wayside shops, newspaper selling, coolies, shoes-shine boys, vender, etc. Though Indian law does not prohibit the employment of children in cottage industries, family households, restaurants, or in agriculture yet it is quite evident that the working conditions of the children in these small organizations is far inferior to those of large factories.

According to the report prepared by the India Social Institute on Child Labour, 80 per cent of all child labourers belong to the scheduled castes and tribes that have been exploited and marginalized in India for centuries. A major consequence of this "is the deprival of the possibility of education and the consequent upward modality. Thus child labour has become a mode of perpetuating an unjust social system and of ensuring the continued availability of subservient, unskilled, illiterate labourers who do not have the bargaining power to question the system that marginalizes them and deprives them of their right to be human."

In the long list of dubious distinctions India is famous for, child labour comes on the top. The wholesale and unchecked exploitation of children of less than 14 years is a punishable crime under the Indian law. But a selfish and immoral political leadership corrupt bureaucracy, rampant poverty, growing unemployment and a society bereft of values gave all conspired to turn India into the "largest concentration of child labour in the world." In India every third child is working child and every fourth child in the age group 5-15 is employed. An estimate by the international labour organization puts the number of child workers in India at 44 million.But an un-official survey estimates the number of working children at around 100 million. While 21 per cent of the child workers are urban-based, the rest are rural-based.

There is hardly any product in India that has no child labour behind it. Lock, carpet, bangle, brick, match box, cracker wood carvingor any other product has the invisible stamp of the tail put in by children caught in the web of poverty and an exploitative social system. Indeed,child labour in India is comes cheap and easy.

The magnitude of the child labour in India is quite evident form the depicted as under:

Table 1

year	Total population	Total labour force	Total child population	The child labuur
	100.00	100.00	100.00	100.00
1961	438936918	188675500	180082782	14469774
	124.00	95.66	127.90	74.30
1971	548159652	180485006	230334822	10753982

	151.60	117.94	146.10	77.20
1981	665287832	2225!6568	263064491	11168819
1991	836605522	314903522	NA	NA

The study of Table 1, reveals that total population increased by 24.9 per cent in 1971 and 51.6 per cent in 1981 with 1961 as the base year. The table also shows the trends in total child population and child-labour. Child population increased by 27.9 per cant in 1971 and 46.1 per cent in 1981 with 1961 as the base year, which is slightly lower than the increase in total population. Child labour decreased by 25.7 per cant in 1971 and 22.8 per cant in 1981 with 1961 as the base year. During 1971-81 the average child population was 22,44,97,302 and average child was 1,21,30,859,i.e. child labour was 5.66 per cant of total labour force and 2.31 per cant of total population on an average during the period from 1961 to1981.

Similarly, Table 2 throws a flood of light on the different aspects of child labour in India. It shows the percentage change in child labour, total labour force and child population in respect of the total child population, total labour force and total population during 1961-1991.

Table 2

Year	Child labor in total child population	child labor in total population force	child labor in total labor poputaion	child population in total total	Total labor force in population
1961	8.04	3.29	7.67	41.02	42.98
1971	4.69	1.96	5.96	42.02	32.93
1981	4.25	1.68	5.02	39.54	33.45
1991	NA	NA	NA	NA	NA
%age	-3.97	-1.61	-2.65	-1.48	-9.53

It is revealed from table 2, that the share of child labour decreased by 3.79 per cent in total child population, 2.65 per cant in total labour force and 1.61 per cent in total population. The share of total labour force in total population and total child population in total population decreased by 9.53 per cant and 1.40 per cant respectively. From the above analysis we find that the share of child labour is decreasing very slowly in the country, inspite of preventive and protective legislations and the government policy to prevent child employment. The percentage do not seem to be very alarming, but it must be kept in mind that the percentage would be much larger. if we include shoe shine boys, vehicle cleaners, domestic servants children who work in their own house to enable their parents to go out to work, etc. and excluding infants and children below the age of five years from the 0-14 years age group which we took for our analysis.

The high incidence of child labour in India is not only shocking from the moral point of view, but also represent a waste of waste resources, which instead of being improved upon through education and training is utilized in a most unproductive and wasteful manner.

A recent state-wise figure reveals that Andhra Pradesh topped the list with over 19 lakh child labour followed by Madhya Pradesh, Maharashtra, Utter Pradesh, Karnataka and Bihar, each accounting for over two lakh. From this it is quite evident that the employment of children. which is a centuries-old phenomenon in India has given to a number of social,psychological economical and legal problems.

The social evils involves in the employment of children are widespread illiteracy resulting in lack of development of child's personality which may continue even in his adult life. The economic problems involved in the employment of children in agriculture and industrial sectors are in on way of less significance. The inadequacy of family income and desire to supplement family income has compelled children to work in agricultural and industrial sectors. However, employment in such establishments do not provide them adequate wages. The legal problem involved in the employment of children are:(1)what should be their minimum wages?(2)what should be the industries in which they may be employed? (3)what should be the number of their work? (4)what should be the direction of their work? (5)what privilege should be afforded to them in the matter of leave and holidays? (6)what protection should be afforded to them in matter of health, safety and welfare?(7)what securities should be allowed to them in case of their compulsory removal from their work?

It is true that the constitution of India provides that no child below the age of 14 years shall be employed to work in any hazardous employment. Article 15(3)children in the light of philosophy contained in article 39 which states that the tender age of children shall not be abused and that the children are given proper opportunities and facilities to develop in a healthy manner youth are protected against exploitation and against moral and material abandonment. Our national charter further endeavors to provide, within a period of ten years from the commencement of the constitution, for free and compulsory education for all children until they complete the age of 14 years.

Keeping in view the constitutional commitment many legislations have been passed relating to the welfare and special protection of the children. Today we have more then 300 union and state statutes dealing with children on one way and other. In 1974, adopted a National policy for children which begins by saying that the children are supremely important assets of the nation the year 1979 have gone. The world has celebrated the year but the child labour remains. Thus the problem of child labour welfare requires a considerable attention from social scientists, activists on the field and the government.

The problem is more acute particularly in under-developed and developing country like India. It is now a realized and accepted truth that protection of children against exploitation is essential to their mental and physical development and in the ultimate analysis to the development to nation as a whole.Thus the present work is a humble attempt to bring forth some of the legal aspects of this multi-dimensional problem and to give some suggestions for mitigating the acuteness and gravity of this evil.

2

Children in India: A Profile

Definition of a Child

The legal conception of a child depending upon the purpose: whether it is for imposing legal disabilities (in juvenile justice system), for affording protection (from exploitative or hazardous employment), or for establishing eligibility to receive benefits or special services (health, education and maintenance benefits), underlying these alternative definitions are also very different conceptions of the child. These include viewing children as a burden which invoke rights to maintenance and support; regarding children as undergoing temporary disabilities making for rights to special treatment and special discrimination; treating children as specially vulnerable for ensuring rights of protection; and recognizing children as resources for the country's development giving rise of nurturing and advancement. Under different economic and socio-cultural circumstances, the child has also been regarded as a commodity, as an insurance, as a source of labour, and as a social burden.

In India too, the definition of a child varies with the purpose. The Census of India treats persons below the age of fourteen as "children" While making use of standard demographic data, social scientists include females in the age group of 15 to 19 years under the category of the "girl child". According to the constitution, no child below the age of 14 years shall be employed to work in any factory or mine or engaged in any other hazardous employment (Article 23). The legal definition of "child" depends very much upon the specific legislation.

Definition of a Child : Illustrations from the Law in India

1.Criminal Law (Indian Penal Code, 1860)

Nothing is an offense which is done by a child under seven years of age.

Nothing is an offense which is done by a child above seven years of age under twelve, who has not attained sufficient maturity of understanding to judge the nature and consequence of his conduct on that occasion.

(Section 83)

2.Juvenile Law:The Juvenile Justice Act, 1986

"Juvenile" is a boy who has not attained the age of sixteen years, and a girl who has not attained the age of eighteen years.

3.Family Law: Child Marriage Restraint Act, 1929

"Child" means a person who, if a male, has not completed twenty one years of age, and if a female, has not completed eighteen years of age.

4.Labour Laws:Apprentices Act, 1951

A person shall not be qualified to engaged as an apprentice.... unless he is not less than fourteen years of age.

5.Factories Act, 1948

No child who has not completed his fourteenth years shall be required or a allowed to work in any factory.

6.Mines (Amendment) Act, 1983

No person below eighteen years of age shall be allowed to work in any mine or part thereof.

7.The Child Laboul (Prohibition and Regulation) Act, 1986

"Child" means a person who has not completed his fourteenth years of age.

Situation of Indian Children and their Rights

Existing constitutional provisions, policy framework, legislation and above all the commitment at the highest government level gives an impetus to the efforts being made to meet the basic needs of children. Over the years, with the launching of sophisticated techniques with long-term benefits for the welfare and development of children, there is a marked improvement in the situation of children. It is encouraging to note that we have reached a stage where the country has the ability to cater to the basic needs of children, which are relevant for promoting holistic development and full realization of the child's potential. The Convention on the Rights of the Child (CRC) has facilitated conversion of these basic needs of the children into their normative rights. The Government of India, by rectifying the Convention has accepted the provisions made in the articles of the Convention.

India's National Plan of Action for Children aims to improve the situation of children by the turn of the century. The Plan is based on an understanding of the present situation of children and the available facilities, resources, etc.

In India, a person below 14 years of age is considered as a child Accordingly, all programmes for children are geared towards this age group. Even the age specific child related demographic and vital statistics made available by the Census of India, sample Registration Systems and Statistical organizations focus on this age group 0-14 years.

Article 1 of the Convention states that "for the purposes of the present convention, a child means every human being below the age of 18 years, unless, under the law applicable to the child, majority is attained earlier".

The acceptance of this definition is likely to have implications on programme planning and budgetary provisions. The Government of India is therefore reviewing the legislation and is considering adopting the definitions of the child as stated in Article 1 of the Convention, wherever it is feasible and applicable, so that the rights of children are protected in the society under all circumstances.

Another important aspect related to planning programmes for children is the availability of data related to vital events. Both Article 7 and Article 8 of the convention emphasize on immediate registration after birth, the right to a name and nationality. Article 7 states that "the child shall be registered immediately after birth and shall have the right from birth to a name, the right to acquire a nationality and, as far as possible, the right to know and be cared for by his or her parents."

Further Article 8 states that "States Parties undertake to respect the right of the child to preserve his or her identity, including nationality, name and family relations as recognized by law without unlawful interference".

In our country, there is a regular system of registration of births; deaths and names. The Office of the Registrar General of India, under the Ministry of Home Affairs is responsible for registering the birth and name of the new borns.

The work of registration of births and deaths in the country is governed by the provisions in the Registration of Births and Deaths Act, 1969 (RBD) and the rules framed there upon by various State Governments between 1970 and 1982.

Under the Act, registration of all births occurring in the country has been made compulsory and free of charge, if reported within the prescribed time-limit. At present, the period prescribed for the registration of birth varies from 14 to 21 days in various parts of the country. Section 13 of the Act also has provision for delayed registration for events which would not be registered within the normal reporting period. Under Section 12 of this Act, the first copy of the extracts of registration, which is also known as birth certificate is given free of charge.

The necessary reporting form prescribed for the birth registration of a new born contains an item on name of the child. Quite after this information is not provided at the time of birth registration. Accordingly, there exists a provision in the RBD Act 1969 (Section 14), under which the parent or guardian of the child can give information regarding the name of the child to the Registrar either orally or in writing within a prescribed time which can be entered in the register.

As registration of these vital events and availability of this data in time are crucial for planning the various development programmes, concerted efforts are being made to create awareness for cent per cent timely registration of new borns, especially in the case of deliveries at home in urban slums, rural and tribal areas.

The Government of India considers all the children as the nation's supremely important asset. However, in spite of the fact that the concept of gender equality has been basic to Indian thinking for over a century, the girl child has remained neglected. The Indian constitution has granted equality to women and empowered the state to adopt measures of affirmative discrimination in favour of women. The National Policy for Children also stresses on providing equal opportunities for development of children so as to reduce inequality and ensure social justice. Even in the struggle of human rights in the past two decades, undivided attention has been bestowed upon children and women. However, all these developmental efforts have not reached the girl child to the desired extent. This is so, because in all these attempts at national and international level, the development of the girl child has remained subsumed within the larger framework of woman and child development.

In order to accord to the girl child her rightful share of opportunity and status, the World Summit for Children singled out with urgency the situation of the girl child and called for her equitable development. Article 2 of the convention guarantees the right of equality to the children irrespective of their sex. It states that "State Parties shall respect and ensure the rights set forth in the present convention to each child within their jurisdiction without discrimination of any kind, irrespective of the child's or his or her parents or legal guardians race, colour, sex, language, religion, political or other opinion, national, ethnic or social origin, property, disability, birth or other status......"

In India, even prior to the World Summit, efforts were being made to reduce gender inequality among children now with the formulation of the National Plan of Action for Children and the Action Plan for the SAARC Decade of the Girl Child, vigorous activities are being undertaken to remove the gender bias and improve the status of the girl child in society so as to provide her with equal opportunities for survival and development.

The National Plan of Action aims to promote programmes for the girl child and adolescent girls, which embrace a whole range of activities such as nutrition, education, health, recreation, up gradation of home-based skills, and promotion of her decision-making capability as an adolescent girl, particularly at the village level.

The Action Plan for the SAARC Decade of the Girl Child declares the major goals for child survival, protection and development as the decade goals for the girl child. In addition, the gender-specific SAARC goals include increased efforts for the elimination of gender disparities in infants and under five child mortality rates; special emphasis on raising the present age of marriage by at east two years, and postponement of the first pregnancy till after the age of 20; reduction of related female workload; focus attention to protection of girls from exploitative social environment; and promotion of programmes of both advocacy and action n the developmental areas of health, education, welfare, etc. The main strategic principle in implementing the Decade Plan of Action is to strengthen the awareness and capacity of the family and the community to a point, that the goals for the girl child are owned, pursued and achieved by them with support from the Government agencies across different sectors.

The various Government Departments i.e. Department of Women and Child Development, Department of Family Welfare and Department of Education are giving special emphasis on gender specific intervention and programmes with the support of NGOs.

Since 1991 the Scheme for Adolescent Girls is being implemented by the Department of Women and Child Development using ICDS infrastructure. The scheme is for school drop-out girls in the age group 11-18 years and attempts to make the adolescent girls better future mothers. The interventions introduced fall into two categories. In the first intervention programme, the adolescent girls in the age group 11-15 years belonging to poor families, receive hands on training and experience in Anganwadis in the area of health, nutrition, pre-school education and child care. In the second intervention programme, the adolescent girls in the age group 11-18 years get the opportunities to discuss their problems and get facilities for non-formal education, development of home-based skills, recreation, etc. in Balika Mandals. The scheme is being implemented in 507 ICDS blocks to benefit 4.50 lakh girls. Till June 1993, 2.70 lakh adolescent girls had been covered under the scheme.

The girl child has become the focus of universalization

of primary education in an effort to achieve "Education for All by 2000 A.D." Special emphasis is being given to the enrollment and retention of the girl child under various programmes of the Department of Education.

The Discrimination against girl child before birth is being restrained by protective measures being taken by the State Government. The Maharashtra Assembly passed Pre-natal Diagnostic Techniques Act in 1988 (Maharashtra Act No. XV of 1988) thus banning sex determination test. In the state of Tamil Nadu, the State Government has introduced the Girl Child Protection Scheme which offers the parents Rs. 2,000 in fixed deposit for the second girl child. To be eligible for the scheme the parents should have no son, their annual income should be less than Rs. 6,400 and one of the parents must be sterlised. In addition, the State Government has also launched the Cradle Scheme in 1993 to take care of the abandoned female babies.

All these efforts have resulted in marked awareness to reduce gender inequality. As per 1991 data out of the total female population, about 36 per cent were girls in the age group 0-14 years. The decline in female mortality rates, especially in the age group 0-4 years and 5-15 years indicated improvement in the survival of the girl child. In the age group 0-4 years, the mortality rate declined from 43.3 in 1981 to 27.5 in 1991, while in the age group 5-14 years the decline was from 3.1 in 1981 to 2.2 in 1991.

The social norms of Indian society requires girls to marry early and assume domestic responsibilities. To ensure safe motherhood the Child Marriage Restraint Act (amended in 1978), raising the minimum age of marriage for girls from 15 years came into force. In the last decade, there has been steady increase in the age of marriage for girls from 15.5 years in 1981 to 19.5 years in 1991.

The sex differentials in literacy are still very pronounced, though there has been a marked improvement in the female literacy rate from 29.75 per cent in 1981 to 39.29 per cent in 1991. On the whole enrollment of girls in schools has increased eight fold from 5.4 million in 1950-51 to 44.9 million in 1992-93. In 1992-93, the school enrollment at primary stage was above 100 in many states. The vast increase in school enrollment at the higher levels indicated significant improvement in girl's education which is very important for all round development of women.

In the last decade there has been some improvement in the school drop-out rate of girls, though the figure continues to be quite high. It is estimated that about 50 per cent of the girls enrolled at the primary stage drop-out before finishing primary school.

In the present context integrated and holistic approach has to be used to reduce gender inequality. Concerted efforts have to be made to make the girl child enter the mainstream of economic and social activity and to walk out of the maza of neglect in which she has been lost for centuries. This will require massive advocacy and social mobilization, starting from the highest political level using all channels of communication.

Article 24 of the Convention on the Rights of the Child states with urgency the child's right to be enjoyment of the highest attainable standards of health. Again article 6 of the Convention asserts that the State should recognize that every child has the inherent right to life.

In the Indian context, health is a constitutional mandate. The National Health Policy (1983) has given highest priority to launching special programmes for the improvement of maternal and child health. As a result care of mothers and children ha been given utmost priority in the health service delivery system. India is committed to attain the goal of Health for All by 2000 AD through universal provision of comprehensive primary health care services. Most of the targets set to achieve this goal are related to health of children and women.

The data regarding child population by age group in India and projection of child population from 1986-2001 are present in Table 1. The table reveals that there is a tremendous increases in the child population over the period under reference. It has also been estimated that by 2001 A.D. the total population of children below 14 years will become 3,07,168,000. The same statistics for different states are given in Table 2. It is evident from the table that U.P. is having maximum child population followed by Bihar and Maharashtra. The minimum population has been noticed in the states of Haryana, Punjab followed by Kerala and Assam.

Table 1 : Child Population by Age Group in India and Projection of Child Population from 1986-2001

(Population in '000)

Sl. No.	Year	Child Population is the age group (yrs)			
		0-4	5-9	10-14	0-14
1.	1971	79,550	82,007	68,768	2,30,335
2.	1981	97,086	92,145	82,769	2,72,000
3.	1986	*1,05,373	92,096	91,097	2,88,566
4.	1991	*1,05,705	1,00,815	91,229	2,97,749
5.	1996	*1,05,730	1,01,916	1,00,050	3,07,696
6.	2001	*1,03,161	1,02,161	1,01,321	3,07,163

Note: * Relates to medium projections

Sources: 1. *Report of the Expert Committee on Population for India upto 2001-Tables 1.3 and 4.3*

2. *Census of India, 1971 and 1981*

The infant mortality rate is the indicator of development of any country. However, the data in this regard are present in Table 3 which exhibit that Kerala is having the minimum infant mortality rate followed by Tamil Nadu. On these contrary, Orissa followed by M.P. and U.P. are having the maximum IMR. The National Plan of Action for Children given priority to maternal and child health and the targets set are in consonance with those of Health for All. The major child health goal of the Plan is to reduce infant mortality rate (IMR) to below 60 and child mortality rate to below 10 per thousand.

The objectives set to achieve this goal include maintenance of immunization coverage at a level of 100 per cent, eradication of polio by 2000 A.D. elimination of neonatal tetanus by 1995, prevention of 95 per cent deaths and 90 per cent cases of measles by 1995, prevention of 70 per cent deaths and 25 per cent cases of diarrhoea and prevention of 40 per cent deaths due to acute respiratory infections (ARI) by 2000 A.D. The major goal of the Plan related to maternal health is reduction of MMR by half between 1990 and 2000 A.D. For this special attention is being paid to health and nutrition of the female child and expectant and nursing mothers, along with expansion and strengthening of existing health programmes in terms of material, facilities, trained manpower, etc.

The Maternal and Child Health (MCH) Programme has been an integrated part of the primary health care services.Under the Under the programmes efforts are being made to promote registration of pregnant women with a view to ensure at least three ante-natal check-ups, immunization and intake of iron and folic acid tablets. The specific programmes of the Ministry of Health and Family Welfare geared towards maternal and child health are Universal Immunization Programme, Oral Rehydration Therapy, and Prophylactic Schemes against Nutritional Anaemia among Pregnant women and against Blindness due to vitamin A deficiency.

As National Health Policy seeks to achieve 100 per cent deliveries by trained personal . Traditional Birth Attendants are being trained and clean delivery is being promoted at all levels. Besides this, birth timing and interval are being promoted as a health measure for both mothers and their children.

The ongoing MCH programmes of the country has been strengthened by launching child survival and safe Motherhood

Programme in 1992-93. The Programme is being implemented in phases so as to cover all districts in the country by 1996-97. The programme is directed towards strengthening immunization, orally rehydration therapy, prephylactic programmes and improving maternal and neo-natal care at the community level. The additional interventions of the programme are expansion of the Programme for Control of Acute Respiratory Infections for children below 5 years of age and setting up a network of First Referral units for improving emergency obstetric care. These interventions will be expanded in a phased manner in six states.

To maximize the reach of health services, there has been increase in the number of PHCs and sub-centres. At present, a network of 21,040 PHCs, 1,31,471 sub-centres and 2,297 Community Health Centres provide the health services.

The development of health facilities and use of integrated approach of packaging maternal and child health care with nutrition, education, water and sanitation, etc. has paid dividends. The impact of these interventions is becoming perceptible in the declining trends of disease incidence and mortality rates. There has been significant progress in the infant mortality rate, for a level of 119 deaths per 1000 live births in 1981 to 79 in 1992. The age specific child mortality rate has also declined for all age groups, the decline being substantial in the age group 0-4 years and 5-14 years. In the age group 0-4 years, the decline was from 41.2 in 1981 to 26.5 in 1991, whereas in the age group 5-14 years the mortality rate declined from 2.9 in 1981 to 2.1 in 1991. However, the maternal mortality rate (MMR) is still high, mainly due to anaemia, haeusorrhage, toxemia of pregnancy and septic abortion.

The improvement in the survival of children can also be attributed to successful coverage of all districts for immunization. The achievements by March 1993 ware 90 per cent immunization in three antigens, DPT, DPV and BCG; 86 per cent in measles and 79 per cent in TT for expectant mothers.

There was a reduction in deaths due to diarrhoea of new born babies from 9.5 per cent in 1983 to 9.00 per cent in 1990.

Neo-natal tetanus remains a problem in States which have a high proportion of deliveries conducted by untrained personnel. To resolve the problem, immunization of pregnant women is being stepped up and an intensive programme of training/retaining of all traditional birth attendants has been started from 1994. It is envisaged that the goal of elimination of neo-natal tetanus (NNT) by 1995 by will also be achieved in 11 states and UTs. Likewise, the elimination of polio will also be achieved in a phased manner by 2000 A.D. On the whole, 11 States and UTs are likely to achieve 'Nil' clinical cases of polio myelitis by 1995. In the case of measles, compared to the incidence in 1987, 80 per cent decline has been achieved in 1993.

Attainment of the optimum level of survival and development of children require augmented efforts, including massive advocacy and community empowerment through health related knowledge to achieve the targets set in the National Plan of Action. In addition, the degree to which the child's right to health is being protected also needs due consideration.

Nutrition is seldom mentioned as a human right in UN declarations and conventions. However, in Article 24 and Article 27 of CRC nutrition is explicitly mentioned. Article 24 states that "States parties shall take appropriate measures : to combat disease and malnutrition, including within the framework of primary health care, through, inter alia, the application of readily available technology and through the provision of adequate nutritious food and clean drinking water to ensure that all segments of society, in particular parents and children, are informed, have access to education and are supported in the use of basic knowledge of child health and nutrition, the advantages of breast feeding, hygiene and environmental sanitation."

In Article 27 the emphasis is on supporting nutrition programmes. It states that "....States Parties in accordance with national conditions and within their means, shall take appropriate measures to assist parents and others responsible for the child to implement this right and shall in case of need provide material assistance and support programmes, particularly with regard to nutrition.....

The elimination of child malnutrition can be justified as an investment in human capital but it has above all ethical justification. The nutrition goal agreed upon at the World Summit represent a "moral minimum" and a recognition that it is unethical to allow children to be malnourished and even die of hunger, when we have both, the knowledge and the resources needed to prevent the tragedy.

The Government of India, through various nutrition interventions has been able to reduce the extent and magnitude of malnutrition among children and women arising mainly due to socio-economic deprivation. Though there has been a drop in the population below the poverty line from 37.4 per cent in 1983-84 to 29.2 per cent in 1987-88, about 250 million people still suffer from various degrees of malnutrition. Among the various nutrition intervention programmes being implemented and introduced to address the problem of malnutrition and micro-nutrient deficiencies, the Integrated Child Development Service Programme of the Department of Women and Child Development is the largest nutrition intervention programme launched in 1975 with 33 project, the programme has expanded to 3,381 projects covering rural, urban and tribal areas. The strategy adopted in ICDS is delivery of an integrated package of early childhood services, so that their synergistic effect helps in realizing the objectives of the programme.

The ICDS package of services included supplementary nutrition, immunization, health check-up and referral services to children below 6 years and to expectant and nursing mothers; non-formal pre-school education to children 3-6 years; and nutrition and health education to women. The

Nutrition Component of the package include supplementary nutrition, and health education and prophyaxis against nutritional anaemia and Vitamin A deficiency. The supplementary food is provided to needy children and expectant and nursing mothers to meet one one-third of their daily calorie and protein requirements. As per the latest report (June 1994), 17.3 million children and 3.7 million expectant and nursing mothers receive supplementary nutrition. The programme has brought desirable changes in the nutritional status of children (National Evaluation of ICDS, NIPCCD, 1992). Seeing the impact of the programmes, it is planned to expand nutrition intervention through ICDS, so as to cover all the vulnerable children in the age group 0-6 years.

The programmes of the Food and Nutrition Board (FNB) of the Department of Women and Child Development are directed towards improving the nutrition of the people through a combination of measures such as Nutrition Education and Extension; Development and Promotion of Nutritious Foods; and Fortification of Foods. The nutrition education activities include nutrition demonstration programmes; training in home-scale preservation of fruits and vegetables; orientation in integrated nutrition education; monitoring supplementary feeding at anganwadis; networking with NGOs for nutrition education and mass media communication; and celebration of National Nutrition Week, World Food Day and World Breast Feeding Week. During April to November 1993, 1730 nutrition demonstration programmes were organized.

The other nutrition intervention programmes of the Department of Women and Child Development are Special Nutrition Programme, Balwadi Nutrition Programme, Wheat Based Supplementary Nutrition Programme, Tamil Nadu Integrated Nutrition Programme and Mid Day Meal Programme for School Children. The intervention programmes of the Department of Family Welfare for combating specific nutrition deficiency disease are National Goitre Control Programme, National Iodine Deficiency Disorders Control Programme,

Anaemia Prevention and Control Among Pregnant Women, and Prevention and Control of Vitamin A Deficiency Among Children.

In order to promote breast feeding and ensure proper use of infant foods, the Government of India has adopted National code for Protection and Promotion of Breast Feeding in December 1993. The Code envisages that there will be no advertising or other from of promotion of infant milk foods, feeding bottles and teats. To give effect to the provision of the code, the Infant Milk substitutes Feeding Bottles and Infant Foods (Regulation of Production, Supply and Distribution) Act, 1992 has been enacted. The Act has come into force with effect from 1st August, 1993.

With the formulation of the National Plan of Action, efforts are being made to achieve the major goal of reducing severe and moderate malnutrition among under five children by half of 1990 levels, by 2000 A.D. The objectives set to achieve this goal besides reducing malnutrition are reduction in incidence of low birth weight babies and iron deficiency anaemia in women, control of iodine and Vitamin A deficiency disorders, growth monitoring empowerment of women to breast feed their children, and dissemination of knowledge and support services to increase food production to ensure household food security.

The Government of India has also adopted the National Nutrition Policy in 1993 to tackle the problem of malnutrition, both through direct nutrition interventions for specially vulnerable groups as well as through various conditions for improved nutrition. The nutrition goals in the policy are in consonance with the nutrition goals and objectives of the National Plan of Action.

To implement the National Nutrition Policy , a task force for developing a model for national nutrition surveillance system has been set up. The Inter-ministerial Coordination Committee set up in the Department of Women and Child Development is currently engaged in reviewing the nutritional consideration in the related sectors in line with the objectives of the National Nutrition Policy. The Department has also set up a Data Bank on Nutrition to act as a store house of all vital information on nutrition available in different sectors. The Standing Committee set up in the Department is also actively engaged in the task of working out a National Plan of Action on Nutrition. A National Nutrition Council with the Prime Minister as President has been constituted to oversee the effective implementation of the National Nutrition Policy.

These inputs by the Government have resulted in a significant change in the nutrition scenario of the country. On the whole, there has been a striking decline in clinical forms of severe malnutrition and under-five child mortality. Kwashiorkor, Marasmus and Keratomalasia which used to be major public health problems till the 1960s have almost disappeared. An analysis of Indian nutritional status shows that there has been increase in the average intake of calories even at the lowest income group level, though there has not been a commensurate increase in the consumption of protein, fats and oils. There has also been some improvement in the growth profile of pre-school children. However, as per the NNMB survey (1988-89) only 9.9 per cent children (1-5 years) are normal, 43.8 per cent suffer from moderate degree of PEM and 8.7 per cent from extreme form of malnutrition.

The micro nutrient deficiencies among children and women, though still prevalent are on the decline. As per the research data (NIN), roughly 56 per cent pre-school children and almost 50 per cent of the expectant mothers in the third trimester of pregnancy suffer from iron deficiency. According to NNMB Survey (1989-90), there has been a marginal decline of 1.8 mg/CH in the mean iron intake, though it has increased in a few States. It is reported that no state in India is free from iodine deficiency. Nearly 40 million persons are suffering from goiter. It is estimated that 2.2 million children are affiliated with criticism, and about 6.6 million are mildly related and suffer from various degrees of motor handicaps. On the whole, iodine deficiency accounts for 90,000 still births and neo-natal deaths every year. NNMB Survey (1988-90) has pointed out low intake of vitamin A in all the States. It has been estimated that nearly 60,000 children become blind every year due to Vitamin A deficiency.

In the next few years vigorous efforts would be made at all levels of society to respect, protect, facilitate and fulfill nutrition rights. Emphasis will be laid on advocacy and community empowerment; development of need based nutrition communication material to create awareness about nutrition problems and their solution amongst the general public; convergence of services by strengthening linkages between the concerned sectors like agriculture, food, health, women and child development, education, rural development, urban development, etc; and linkage of nutrition education with activities like immunization, ORT, promotion of breast feeding, birth spacing, female education etc.

Table 2 : Projected Child Population (0-14 yrs.) by Sex in India and Major States, 1981-2001

Figure in (000)

Sl. No.	Inida State	1981		1986		1991		1996		2001	
		M	F	M	F	M	F	M	F	M	F
1	2	3	4	5	6	7	8	9	10	11	12
	All India	140.32	131.679	148.151	140.415	152,784	144,965	157,996	149,670	157,606	149,556
1.	A. P.	10.370	10,136	10.787	10.617	10,792	10,528	11.240	10,882	10,911	10.553
2.	Assam	4.475	4.215	4.850	4.547	5.000	4,794	5.288	5,035	5.459	5,186
3.	Bihar	14,941	14,209	15.912	15.370	16.497	16,059	18.157	17,529	19,100	18.612
4.	Gujarat	6.876	6,475	7,067	7,050	6.734	6.789	6.889	6.612	6,554	6.297
5.	Haryana	2.830	2.531	3,089	2,815	3.195	2.932	3.179	2,907	2,828	2,588
6.	Karnataka	7.412	7,285	878	7,675	8.081	7.758	8,127	7.723	7.710	7.366
7.	Kerala	4.505	4.454	4.632	4,498	4.686	4.528	4.707	4,500	4,613	4,474
8.	M.P.	10.869	10.418	11.655	11.140	12.139	11.391	12.689	11.864	12.263	11,501
9.	Maharashtra	12.179	11.592	12.630	11,970	12,135	11.474	11.839	11.078	11.474	10.731
10.	Orissa	5.246	5.243	5,456	5,344	5,518	5.258	5,707	5,369	5.651	5.318
11.	Punjab	3.277	2.927	3.378	3.056	3.228	2.965	3.016	2.825	2,808	2.650

12.	Rajasthan	7.527	7,074	8,418	7,930	9,239	8,746	10,231	9,724	10,806	10,293
13.	Tamil Nadu	8,537	8,295	8,804	8,480	8,866	8,486	8,886	8,475	8.602	8,192
14.	Uttar Pradesh	24,907	21,929	26,784	24,061	28,150	25,605	30,418	27,974	32,244	29,944
15.	West Bangal	10,704	10,483	11,111	10,840	11,352	11,030	11,714	11,176	11.352	10,801

Source: Census of India 1981, Occasional papers No.4 of 1988, Report of the Expert Commitee on the Population Projections.

3

Rights of the Child

The most valuable of a nation's resources is its children. The nation that fails to ensure the survival, protection and development of its children is doomed to destruction. nay extinction. No nation can, therefore, afford to leave this supreme assert—the children—at the mercy and caprice of individuals.

In India the post-independence era has experienced an unequivocal expression of the commitment of Government to the cause of children through constitutional provisions, policies, programmes, legislations, etc. The constitution of India in Article 39 of the Directive, Principles of State Policy that "the state shall, in particular, direct its policy towards securing... that the health and strength of workers, men and women, and the tender

age of children are not abused, and that of citizens are not forced by economic necessity to enter avocation unsuited to their age or strength, that children are given opportunities and facilities to develop in a healthy manner, and in condition of freedom and dignity,and that childhood and youth are protected against exploitation,and against moral and material abandonment.

As a follow-up of this commitment and being a party to UN Declaration on the Right of the 1959, India adopted the National Policy on children in 1974. The policy reframed the constitutional provision and states that "it shall be the policy of the state to provide adequate services to children, both before and birth and through the period of growth to ensure their full physical, mental and social development.The State shall progressively increase the scope of such servicer so that within a reasonable time all children in the country enjoy optimum conditions for their balanced growth."

As the responsibility of children's nurture and solicitude is bestowed on the Government, children's programmes have occupied a prominent palace in the national plans for human resource develoment. Successive Five Year Plans have provided the wherewithal to deal with these issues.In the last decade of this century, dramatic technological developments particularly in the areas of health, nutrition, education and related spheres have opened up new vistas of opportunities to reaffirm our age-old pledges for the cause of children.

During 1989-90, India joined the committee of nations in the successive reaffirmations of global commitment to the cause of children. The UN Convention on the Rights of the child (20 November 1989), the World Conference on Education for all (March 1990) the Global consultation on Water and Sanitation (September 1990), the World Summit on Children (September 1990) and the SAARC Summit on Children soon after the World Summit were part of this redeeming process which transcended national barriers.

Historical Perspective

The 20th century has witnessed world-wise efforts made

to create an environment in which all the children are able to live securely and realize their full potential.As a result,today there are more than 80 international laws, covenants and declaration setting out human rights of children.

In 1959, the UN General Assembly unanimously adopted the Declaration on the Right of Child,10 principles that assert that making owes to the child the best it has to give.Since then, the Declaration has been the guiding framework for children's right. On 20th November 1989, the thirtieth anniversary of this Declaration, the UN General Assembly adopted the Convention on the Rights of the Child drafted by the UN commission on Human Rights.The convention came into force as an international law on 2nd September 1990, following ratification by the stipulated minimum of 20 member states.It is envisaged that the end of 1995, all countries of the world would ratify the convention .

The convention consisting of 54 articles,is derived from a basic set of values and ethical premises that recognize the inherent dignity and the equal and inalienable rights of all member of the human family as the foundation of freedom,justice and peace in the world. It is a set of international standards and measures that intends to protect and promote the well being of children in society. The convention provides the legal basis for initiating action to ensure the rights of children in society.

The convention drawn attention to the rights of children related to their survival,protection and development. The Right to Survival includes the right to life,the highest attainable standard of health,nutrition and adequate standards of living.It also includes the right to a name from birth, the right to acquire a nationality and as far as possible, the right to know and be cared for by her parents. The Right to Protection not only includes freedom from all from of exploitation, inhuman or degrading treatment and neglect, but also the right to special protection in situation of emergency and armed conflicts.The Right to Development includes the right to edu cation, support for early childhood development and care, social security,and the right to leisure, recreation and cultural activities.The Right to participation includes respect for the views of child, freedom of expression, access to appropriate information, and freedom of thought, conscience and religion.

The Convention was strongly endorsed by the World Summit on children held on 30th September 1990.In fact, this was the first major global action for the implementation of the convention. The World Summit adopted the Declaration on the Survival, Protection and Development of children along with a Plan of Action for implementing the Declaration. Together the Declaration and plan of Action of the World Summit for children and the convention on the Rights of the Child constitute for ambition and focussed agenda for the well being of children to be achieved by the year 2000. In committing themselves to pursuing these goals, the leaders of world have agreed to guided by principle of a"First call for Children" —a principle that the essential needs of children should be given high priority in the allocation resources, in bad time as well as in the good times and at national, international as well as at family levels . As a part of the Plan of Action for implementing the World Declaration major and sectoral goals were formulated.All the Governments were urged to prepare their own National Plans of Action by 1991, to achieve the targets set in these goals with appropriate adaptation to the specific of each country in terms of standards, priorities and availability of resources keeping in mind the cultural, religious and social traditions.

The Convention

The convention on the Rights of the Child, drafted by the UN Commission on Human Rights and adopted by the General Assembly of the United National on 20th November 1989,is a set of international standards and measures intended to protect and promote the well being of children in society.As of 1993,159 countries had either signed the convention or become state parties to it by rectification, accession or succession,the goal being that by the end of 1995, all countries of the world have notified the Convention. The Convention recognizes the exceptional vulnerability of children, and proclaims that childhood is entitled to special case and assistance.It is guided by the principle of "First call for children"a principle that the essential needs of children should be given highest priority in the allocation of resources at all times It obligates the state to respect and ensure that children get a fair and equitable deal in society.It emphasizes the importance of the family and need to an environment that is conductive to the healthy growth and development of children.It advocates concerted public action by individuals and agencies —government as well as non-governmental, local, national, regional and international to promote the rights of the child.The Convention,in a sense,is a means of empowering children and creating an environment in which all children are able to live securely and realize their full potential in life.

The Convention draws attention to four of civil,political, social,economic and cultural rights of every child.These are:

1. The right to survival
2. The right to protection
3. The right to development
4. The right to participation

The Convention provides the legal basis for initiating action to ensure the rights of children in society.

India and the Convention

To an extent, the Convention reiterates and elaborates what is already contained in the Constitution of India.According to Article 39 of the Directives Principles of State Policy :

The state shall, in particular, direct its policy towards securing :

1. That the health and strength of workers,men and women and the tender age of children are not abused and that citizen are not forced by economic necessity to enter avocations un-

suited to their age or strength;

2. That children are given opportunities and facilities to develop in a healthy manner and in conditions of freedom and dignity and that children and youth are protected against exploitation and against moral and material abandonment.

The National Policy for Children in 1974 affirmed the constitutional Provisions and declared that "it shall be the policy of the state to provide adequate services to children,both before and after birth and through the period of growth, to ensure their full physical,mental and social development.The state shall progressively increase the scope of such services so that, within a reasonable time,all children in the country enjoy optimum conditions balanced growth".

Government of India, by ratifying the Convention on the Right of the child on November 12,1992,once again its commitment to children. This obligates the Government to :

* review national and state legislation and bring it in line with the provisions of Convention ;

* develop appropriate monitoring procedures to assess progress in implementing the convention ;

* involve all relevant government, Ministers and department, international agencies, non-governmental organization, and the legal profession in the implementation and reporting process;

* publicize the convention and seek public input for reporting; and

* ensure that reporting is frank transparent.

Definition of a Child

According to the Convention:"....a child means every human being below the age of eighteen years unless, the law applicable to the child, majority is attained earlier".

Rights of the child

1.The Right to Survival

The problem of overcoming avoidable child deaths continues to plague several countries of the world.The fact that children die in this day and age when there are simple and cost-effective solutions to prevent escapable mortality is a matter of shame. UNICEF's Executive Director, Mr. James Grant, addressing the Executive Board in June 1993, remarked :

"....I now take the liberty,with your permission,of asking the Executive Board to observe a moment of silent for the 40,000 children who,dyeing this day largely from preventable and environmental causes, are losing their chance to enjoy the potential benefits and opportunities of Mother Earth—and for the 40,000 who lost that chance yesterday and the 40,000 children who will it tomorrow and everyday.These deaths are not ultimate waste of the most precious resources of our planet,but as we learn how to prevent they are increasingly becoming an obscenity.Morality marches with changing capacity ."

The convention places primary emphasis on the right of every child to avoid escapable mortality and morbidity,and to he-

althy life .

The Convention state: State parties recognize that every child has the inherent right to life . (Article 6)

Child Mortality in India

Most recent estimates place India's infant mortality rate (IMR) at 79 and the under five mortality rate at 124 per 1000 live births 90 countries out of 145 had a lower infant mortality rate (U5 MR) than India's and 103 countries a lower under five mortality rate.

These included developing countries such as Botswana,

Kenya, Zimbabwe, Egypt, Morocco, Sri Lanka, Vietnam, Indonesia and with the exception of Haiti, all countries in Central and South America and the Caribbean.

India has made progress in reducing its infant mortality rate from a level of 129 deaths per 1000 live births in 1971 to 1979 in 1992.Yet, of the million children born every year in India, two million die before reaching the age of one. A majority of these deaths are due to avoidable infection and malnutrition.

Children in India continue to face unequal chances of survival depending upon where they are born.For example,infant mortality ranges from 17 per 1000 live birth in Kerala to 144 in Orissa.If all of India had Kerala's child birth and death rates, some 10 million fewer children would be born and some 1.76 million fewer children would every year.

Also, infant mortality in rural areas has always exceeded the IMR in urban areas, and the gap continues to persist. For instance the IMR in rural areas (86) in 1990 was higher than IMR attained in urban areas twenty years ago (82 in 1971), and is much higher than current IMR levels in urban areas estimated to be 51 per 1000 live births.

This does not however,imply that child survival condition in urban ares are uniformly superior to those prevailing elsewhere in the country.An estimated 38.8 million people live below the poverty line in urban areas,and it is estimated that 15 to 16 million children live in condition of acute deprivations with inadequate access to basic health care, nutrition, safe drinking water,and education.Moreover, the reported high prevalence of HIV sero—positivity among urban prostitutes which marks populations living in urban slums particularly vulnerable to the spread of AIDS.

Chances of children surviving also vary with the socio-economic background of parents.For instance, the estimated 45 MR in 1981 among infants of rural woman who worked as agricultural was 193; the corresponding figure for those engaged in non-manual employment was only 106.Again in the category of manual woman workers in rural areas, the 45 MR estimated for 1981 ranged from 388 in Orissa to 109 in Kerala.

Health Services

There has a steady expansion in the provisioning of public health and medical services in the country.As a result,children too have benefited.In 1992 for instance, the proportion of one year old children reported to be immunized against DPT was 89 per cent, against measles 85 per cent,and against polio was 90 per cent. The achievements, however, have not been equally impressive in all fields.For example,provider compliance with use of Oral dehydration Salts for treatment of diarrhea remains very low and at 12 per cent; and use of ORT is estimated to be 37 %.

Access to and utilization of health and medical services by children have tended to vary across the country depending upon the costs, quality, and levels of public provisioning as well as the effectiveness of demand for such services. While not many studies have focussed on the relationship of costs and quality to access and utilization,provisioning in urban areas is undoubtedly better than in rural area. For instance,while 53 per cent of children born in urban areas received medical attention in institution like hospitals,maternity nursing homes and health centres,the corresponding figure for rural areas was only 16 per cent.Again while in Kerala, 90 per cent of children received attention in such institution at the time of birth,only four per cent of children born in Uttar Pradesh received similar attention.

Studies on the health status of children in India have also repeatedly pointed to the importance of woman's achievements, and that of mothers in particular.Health seeking behavior among women and children is better among communities where women are more literate and educated,and have greater freedom to participate in economic activities outside the household.However, women's access to health facilities are often found to be constrained byvarious socio-cultural factors.Thus,in addition to focusing on improving public provisioning of basic servicer,and enhancing the incomes of the poor to avail of the services,are also needed to address caste class, and gender issues that restrict utilization of services in India.

Nutrition

Government of India's National Policy (1993) draws attention to the serious problems of malnutrition among children in the country. Even though there has been a drop in the population below the poverty line to 29.2 per cent in 1987-88,in terms of numbers, a staggering 250 million people presently suffer from varying degrees of malnutrition in India.

Recent studies also point out that children in urban slums and poor neighborhood in urban areas live under particularly vulnerable condition of health and nutritional well-being. The risk of a slums child receiving a calorie deficient diet, for instance,is reported to be twice as high as compared to those of children from middle income and low income families.Government of India has taken several steps to the problem of malnutrition. The Integrated Child Development Services (ICDS) launched in 1975 has expanded to become the largest nutrition programme in the world with 3,066 projects covering 16.2 million children in the age group of to 6 years and million pregnant women.The packages of services provided under this programme includes supplementary feeding immunization,health check-up,referral services, non-formal pre-school education and nutrition and health education.India's performance in terms of food production has also been impressive over the last few years,with record level of 180 million tones of food grain produced in 1992-93. The country has built up a food buffer stock of million tones, and has in place a network of more than 400,000 fair shop for public distribution of essential commodities to the poor at lower than market prices.Despite these and programmes like the use of ORT and universal immunization,nutritional deprivation and hunger are the norms,with over 43.8% (1988-90) children suffering from moderate malnutrition and about 37.6%(1989-90) from mild malnutrition.

Government of India's Nutritional Policy recognizes that nutrition is a multi-sectoral issue, and has called for evolving a mix of both direct nutrition intervention as well as development policy instruments which will create condition of improved nutrition. The Oslo Initiative for a World Alliance for Nutrition and Human Rights observes that "In order to ensure sound nutrition as much has to be given also to child care and protection and promotion of child health as to food security".Efforts to develop more such integrated approaches will need to be reinforced and strengthened.

The Right to Protection

The convention states: State Parties shall take all appropriate legislative, administrative, social and education measures to protect children from all from of physical, mental violence, injury or abuse, neglect or negligent treatment or exploitation, including sexual abuse...... (Article 18) .

Child Labour

Economic exploitation in India is extensive and appears to have increased over the years.The Census of India 1981 estimated that there were 13.17 million child workers (below the age of fourteen) engaged mostly in rural agricultural activities.The National Sample Survey in 1983 estimated that were 17.36 million child workers in the age group of 5 to 15 years. The Operation Research Group placed the figure at 44 million in 1983.Most of these children work under stressful condition in agriculture and other industries, often hazardous.Some are "bounded" and even sold into prostitution.The Planning Commission estimates that there would be around 20 million child worker by the year 2000.

The Convention States: State Parties recognize the right of the child to be protected from economic exploitation and from performing any work that is likely to be hazardous or to interfere with the child's education or to be harmful to the child's health or physical, mental, spiritual, moral and social development. (Article 32).

The prevalence of such high levels of child labour is attributable in good measure to the fact that primary education for children is not compulsory in India.Children who are out of school invariably perform work of some sort,either at home or outside, and any wages that are often exploitative, and under conditions that are clearly harmful.Most of the working children also belong to families that are extremely poor.Parents of such children, the selves deprived of basic education,find it extremely difficult to support their families.Children who work, therefore, are the ones who need education most of all to break out of the poverty and Dwelt trap.

In addition to legislative measures that will make primary education compulsory and hiring of children illegal under all circumstances, undertaking public advocacy and building social awareness should be regarded as critical elements of public action to ensure the elimination of child labour .

Children in Difficult Circumstances

India has several million children living under especially difficult circumstances.These include, for instance, an estimated 500,000 street children in seven cities: Bangalore, Bombay, Calcutta, Deilh, Hyderabad, Kanpur and Madras.The majority of these children are over eight years of age,have never attended school, and have parents who low paid unskilled jobs.Destitute and orphaned children are another group about which very little is known.Similarly, there is very little information available about children of prostitutes, children in institution, children of construction workers, children of fisher folk, disabled children, and children affected by riots and disasters,all of whom fall under the category of "children in especially difficult circumstances". There is also reportedly sale of such children and girl trafficking across regional and national borders.

Policy-makers have long ignored the special needs of such children.The convention makers a strong case for special consideration to protect the rights of these children.

The Right to Development

There are two types of development emergencies which inclued natural desasters and armed conflicts that kill, displace or disable children and, " silent" emergencies resulting from indemic, poverty and Widespred deprivations which lead to many more deaths than famines, flood or war, widespread illiteracy, malnutrtion, hunger, morbidity, Poor health, and neglest of womens concerns are examples of "silent" deprivationsthat have seldom received adequate attention. Prof. John Kenneth Galbraith, while "looking at the larger world and its present problems" in a lecture delivered in New Delhi in November 1992 remarked: ".....Once it was understood: an educated population is the first requirement for economic progress. That essential fact was forgotten: impressive steel mills, hydro-electric dams, glistening air-ports, were too often sited amid ignorant people. I have previously made the point in this world there is no literate population that is than poor.

A pro-children development strategy has to address both these types of emergencies, and also needs to be set in the larger context of the economic development strategy adepted by a country.

Education

Recognizing the need to make available free and universal primary education is not to India. Article 45 of the Directive priniples of State Policy declares: The State shall endeavour to provide wihtin a peroid of ten years from the commencement of this Constitution, for free and compulsory education for all children until they complate the age of fourteeen'. (constitution of India, 1950)

The National Policy on Education (1986) as well as the goals for Education for all in India (1990) reaffirm the country's commitment to universalizing primary education by the year2000.

There has been progress in the provisioning of primary schools over the last forty years:

- the number of recognized primary schools has gone up from 209, 671 in 1951 to 572, 541 in 1993.

- the number of primary school teachers want up from 538,000 in 1951 to 1,637,000 in 1991.

- the enrolment figures in primary schools want up from 19.2 million in 1951 to 99.1 million in 1991.

There has also been a shift in the financeal allocations in favour of education, and within education, in favour of elementary education. For instance, spending on education as a proportion of GNP has risen from about 1.2 percent in 1950-51 to the current level of 3.9 percent. Government is committed to increasing the outlay on education from the current to 6 percent of GNP by the year 2000. During the 1980s, public expenditure on elementary education increased by 4.5 times from Rs. 15,373 million at the beginning of the decade to Rs. 68,883 million in 1989-1990. Expenditure on elementary education today accounts for about 45 percent of the total education budget.

But there is more ground to be covered. While statistics indicate that over 99 million children were enrolled in primary schools in 1990-91, much less is known about attendance, and the quality to education. Data also reveal that:

- an estimated 48 percent of the population remains illiterate today. About 19 to 24 million children in the age group 6-14 and over 121 million adult illiterates in the age group of the 15 to 35 (with over 60 percent females in both cases) are estimated to constitute this group.

- despite the increase in the number of primary schools and teachers, the student-teacher ratio has worsened over the years, from 35.7 in 1950-51 to 60.5 in 1990-91.

- only 52 percent on enrolled primary school children reach Grade V.

There are also several inequities in the system that need to be corrected. For instance, Fewer girls enroll in primary school and more grils than boys drop out before completing Grade V. Also, school drop out rates among children belonging to scheduled castes and scheduled tribes continues to be significantly higher than among children belonging to the rest of the population.

India is one of the few countries in the world where primary education is not comprlsory. As Prof. Myron Wiener Writes.

"....Modern states regard education as a legal duty,not merely as a right: perents are required to sendTheir children to school, children are required to attend school, and the state is obligated to enforcecom pulsory education..... The state thus stands as the ultimate guareian of children, Protection them against both parents and would be employers. This is not the view held in India. Primary education is not compulsory, nor is child labour illegal".

While universalization of primary education and eradication of illiteracy in the age group of 15 to 35 years are basic obfectives of education in the Dighth Five Years Plan(1992-97), a major step in this direction will be to make primary education compulsory. Several other aspects of primary schooling too need to be simultaneously addressed. there is need to step up enrolment particularly among girls, keep children in school, reduce wastage, improve the efficiency of resource use in primary schools, and initiate action to enchance the quality of school education. School hours and the annual calendar hvae to be made flexible to accommodate local needs to parents and children. Above all, the teaching and learning environment has to be made more enjoyable, accurntable and meaningful to children

The Right to Praticipation

Included in the right to participation is the right to accused children, for instance to be treated with dignity in the juvenile justice system. According to the Convention:

"The state shall ensure that no child is arbitrarily detained or Subjected to turture, cruel, inhuman or degrading treatment or punishment, capital punishment or life imprisonment. Accused children have the right to be presumed innocent until proven guilty in a prompt and fair trial to legal or other assistance to be detained separately from adults, to maintain contact with family and to receive a sentence based on rehabilitation rather than punishment".

Limited data available on juvenile crimes for 1991 reveal that 29,591 juveciles were apprehended for various crimes rnder the Indian Penal Code and Local and Special Laws. Most of the juveniles were apprehended on charges of theft, burglary, riots, and under the Prohibition Act and the Gambling Act. Of those apprechended:

- 23,201 Were boys and 6,390 were girls.

- 20 percent were children between the ages of 7 and 12 years, 64 percent were in the age group of 12 to 16 years, and 16 percent were girls in the age group of 16 to 18 years.

- 38 percent were illiterate and 36 percent had complated Primary schooling.

- 70 percent were living with parents another 19 percent with guardians, and only 11 percent were homeless.

- 84 percent were new delinquents and 16 percent were old delinquents.

- 60 percent delonged to females who were earning less than Rs. 500 a mcnth.

Little information, however, is available on the more crucial aspect of treatment meted out to these children. Legal representation of poor children is rate; and very few facilities exist for detention of children separately from adults. Much less is known about the availability and effectiveness of rehabilittion facilities.

Again, children in India, and girls in particular have reportedly little say in the matter of marriage. There are still several thousands of child marriages reported throughout the country. In 1981, for instance, 43 percent of the girls in the age group of 15 to 19 years wer married. Although this proportion varied from 7 percent Goa, Daman and Diu to 64 percent in Rajasthan, early marriages are seldom viewed as a violation of a child's freedom to enjoy children.

Declaration of the Rights of the Child

Proclaimed by the General Assembly of the United Nations on 20 November, 1959 (General Assembly Resolution 1386 XIV)

Preamble

Whereas the peoples of the United Nations have, in the charter, reaffirmed their faith in fundamental human rights and in the dignity and worth of the human person, and have determined to promote social progress and better standards of life in larger freedom.

Whereas the United Nations has, in the Universal Declaration of Human Rights, proclaimed that everyone is entitled to all the rights and freedoms set forth therein, without distinction of any kind, such as race, colour, sex, language, religion, political or other opinion, national or social origin, property, birth or other status.

Whereas the child, by reason of his physical and mental immaturity, needs special safeguards and care, including appropriate legal protection, before as well as after birth.

Whereas the need for such special safeguards has been stated in the Geneva Declaration of the Rights of the Child of 1924, and recognized in the Universal Declaration of Human Rights and in the statutes of specialized agencies and international organizations concerned with the welfare of children.

Whereas mankind owes to the child the best it has to give.Now therefore, The General Assembly proclaims this Declaration of the Rights of the Child to the end that he may have a happy childhood and enjoy for his own good and for the good of society the rights and freedoms herein set forth, and upon voluntary organizations, local authorities and national Governments to recognize these rights and strive for their observance by legislative and other measures progressively taken in accordance with the following principles:

Principle 1

The child enjoy all the rights set forth in this Declaration. Every child, without any exception whatsoever, shall be entitled to these rights, without distinction or discrimination on account of race, colour, sex, language, religion, political or other opinion, national or social origin, property, birth or other status, whether of himself or of his family.

Principle 2

The child shall enjoy special protection, and shall be given opportunities and facilities, by law and by other means, to enable him to develop physically, mentally, morally, spiritually and socially in a healthy and normal manner and in conditions of freedom and dignity. In the enactment of laws for this purpose, the best interests of the child shall be the paramount consideration.

Principle 3

The child shall be entitled from his birth to a name and a nationality.

Principle 4

The child shall enjoy the benefits of social security. He shall be entitled to grow and develop in health; to this end, special care and protection shall be provided both to him and to his mother, including adequate pre-natal and postnatal care. The child shall have the right to adequate nutrition, housing, recreation and medical services.

Principle 5

The child who is physically, mentally or socially handicapped shall be given the special treatment, education and care required by his particular condition.

Principle 6

The child, for the full harmonious development of his personality, needs love and understanding. He shall, wherever possible, grow up in the care and under the responsibility of his parents, and, in any case, in an atmosphere of affection and of moral and material security; a child of tender years shall not, save in exceptional circumstances, be separated from his mother. Society and the public authorities shall have the duty to extend particular care to children without a family and to those without adequate means of support. Payment of State and other assistance towards the maintenance of children of large families is desirable.

Principle 7

The child is entitled to receive education, which shall be free and compulsory, at least in the elementary stages. He shall be given an education which will promote his general culture, and enable him, on a basis of equal opportunity, to develop his abilities, his individual judgment, and his sense of moral and social responsibility, and to become a useful member of society.

The best interests of the child shall be the guiding principle of those responsible for his education and guidance; that responsibility lies in the first place with his parents.

The child shall full opportunity for play and recreation, which should be directed to the same purposes as education; society and the public authorities shall endeavor to promote the enjoyment of this right.

Principle 8

The child shall in all circumstances be among first to receive protection and relief.

Principle 9

The child shall be protected against all forms of neglect, cruelty and exploitation. He shall not be the subject of traffic, in any form.

The child shall not be admitted to employment before an appropriate minimum age; he shall in no case be caused or permitted to engage in any occupation or employment which would prejudice his health or education, or interfere with his physical, mental or moral development.

Principle 10

The child shall be protected from practices which may foster racial, religious and any other form of discrimination. He shall be brought up in a spirit of understanding, tolerance, friendship among peoples, consciousness that his energy and talents should be devoted to the service of his fellow men.

NATIONAL POLICY FOR CHILDREN

RESOLUTION

The Government of India have had under consideration the question of evolving a national policy for the welfare of children. After due consideration, it has been decided to adopt the policy enunciated below:

Introduction

The nation's children are a supremely important asset. Their nurture and solicitude are our responsibility. Children's programme should find a prominent part in our national plans for the development of human resources, so that our children grow up to become robust citizens, physically fit, mentally alert and morally healthy, endowed with the skills and motivations needed by society. Equal opportunities for development to all children, during the period of growth should be our aim, for this would serve our larger purpose of reducing inequality and ensuring social justice.

Goals

The needs of children and our duties towards them have been expressed in the Constitution. The resolution on a national policy on education, which has been adopted by Parliament, gives direction to state policy on the educational needs of children. We are also party to the U.N. declaration of the rights of the child. The goals set out in these documents can reasonably be achieved by judicious and efficient use of the available national resources. Keeping in view these goals, the Government of India adopts this resolution on the national policy for children.

Policy and Measures

It shall be the policy of the state to provide adequate services to children, both before and after birth and through the period growth, to ensure their full physical, mental and social development. The state shall progressively increase the scope of such services so that, within a reasonable time, all children n the country enjoy optimum conditions for their balanced growth. In particular, the following measures shall be adopted towards the attainment of these objectives:

(i) All children shall be covered by a comprehensive health programme.

(ii) Programme shall be implemented to provide nutrition

services with the object of removing deficiencies in the diet of children.

(iii) Programme will be undertaken for the general improvement of the health and for the care, nutrition and nutrition education of expectant and nursing mothers.

(iv) The state shall take steps to provide free and compulsory education for all children upto the age of 14 for which a time-bound programme will be drawn up consistent with the availability of resources. Special efforts will be made to reduce the prevailing wastage and stagnation in schools, particularly in the case of girls and children of the weaker sections of society. The programme of informal education for pre-school children from such section will also be taken up.

(v) Children who are not able to take full advantage of formal school education shall be provided other forms of education suited to their requirements.

(vi) Physical education, games, sports, and other types of recreational as well as cultural and scientific activities shall be promoted in schools, community centres and such other institutions.

(vii) To ensure equality of opportunity, special assistance shall be provided to all children belonging to the weaker sections of the society, such as children belonging to the Scheduled Castes and Scheduled Tribes and those belonging to the economically weaker sections both in urban and rural areas.

(viii) Children who are socially handicapped, who have become delinquent or have been forced to take to begging or are otherwise in distress, shall be provided facilities for education, training and rehabilitation and will be helped to become useful citizens.

(ix) Children shall be protected against neglect, cruelty and exploitation.

(x) No child under 14 years shall be permitted to be engaged in any hazardous occupation or be made to undertake heavy work.

(xi) Facilities shall be provided for special treatment, education, rehabilitation and care of children who are physically handicapped, emotionally disturbed or mentally retarded.

(xii) Children shall be given priority for protection and relief in times of distress or natural calamity.

(xiii) Special programmes shall be formulated to spot, encourage and assist gifted children, particularly those belonging to the weaker sections of society.

(xiv) Existing laws should be amended so that in all legal disputes, whether between parents or institutions, the interests of children are given paramount consideration.

(xv) In organizing services for children, efforts would be directed to strengthen family ties so that full potentialities of growth of children are realized within the normal family, neighborhood and priority in Programming Formation

In formulating programmes in different sectors, priority shall be given to programmes relating to;

(a) preventive and promotive aspects of child health;

(b) nutrition for infants and children in the preschool age along with nutrition for nursing and expectant mothers;

(c) maintenance, education and training of orphan and destitute children;

(d) creches and facilities for the care of children of working or ailing mothers; and

(e) care, education, training and rehabilitation of handicapped children.

Constitution of National Children's Board

During the last two decades we have made significant progress in the provision of services for children on the lines detailed above. There has been considerable expansion in the health, nutrition, education and welfare services. Rise in the standard of living, wherever it occurred, has indirectly met children's basic needs to some extent. But all this work needs of children. A National Children's Board shall be constituted to provide this focus and to ensure at different levels continuous planning, review and coordination of all the essential services. Similar Boards may also be constituted at the state level.

Role of Voluntary Organizations

The Government shall endeavor that adequate resources are provided for child welfare programmes and appropriate schemes are undertaken. At the same time voluntary organizations engaged in the field of child welfare will continue to have the opportunity to develop, either on their own or with State assistance, in the field of education, health, recreation and social welfare services. India has a tradition of voluntary action. It shall be the endeavor of the state to encourage and strengthen voluntary action so that state and voluntary efforts complement each other. The resources of voluntary organizations, should have to be tapped to the extent possible for promoting and developing child welfare programmes.

Legislation and Administrative Action

To achieve the above, the State will provide necessary legislative and administrative support. Facilities for research and training of personnel will be developed to meet the needs of the expanding programmes and to improve the effectiveness of the services.

People's Participation

The Government of India trust that the policy enunciated in this statement will receive the support and cooperation of all sections of the people and of organizations working for children. The Government of India also calls upon the citizens, State Governments, local bodies, educational institutions and voluntary organizations to play their part in the overall effort to attain these objectives.

Secretary to the Government of India.

ORDER

Ordered that a copy of the resolution be communicated to the Cabinet Secretariat, the Prime Minister's Secretariat, all Ministries/Departments of the Government of India, the Planning Commission, the State Governments and the Governments/Administrations of Union Territories.

Order also that the resolution be published in the Gazette of India for general information.

August 22, 1974 Secretary to the Government of India.

THE CHILD IN INDIA

Demographic Profile

Of the 1550 million children in the world, one in every six is in India. The 248 million children of India thus comprise nearly 16 per cent of all the world's children.

India's population is rising faster than the world rate, and the addition of some 13 million infants every year gives India one of the world's youngest populations. The 1971 census showed that 42 per cent of the Indian population consists of children under 14 years of age. Children below 6 years comprise 21 per cent of the population.

An index of the population composition is that while the entire population of India in 1911 was 252 million, projections indicate that children alone already numbered 248 million in 1976, and a more recent estimate puts the child population in 1977 at 255 million. The twentieth century will close with the number of children in India almost certainly exceeding the total Indian population of 279 million recorded in the 1931 Census.

Urban-Rural Ratios: An estimated 81 per cent of India's

children live in the rural areas. According to population projections for 1976, the rural children number 183.9 million, tribal children 14.9 million and urban children 49.7 million. These projections also indicate that nearly half of India's children (48.7 per cent) are below 6 years of age. Of the 121 million in this age group, 89.7 million live in the villages and 7.3 million in tribal areas, while 24.2 million are in urban areas.

Living Conditions: According to 1976 projections, about 99.4 million children-nearly two-fifths of the total Indian child population-live in condition adverse to survival. Of them, 48.5 million, or nearly half, are less than 6 year old.

The 1976 estimates place 35.8 million of these youngest deprived children in rural areas, 9.7 million in urban areas and 2.9 million in tribal areas. In the next age group (7-14 years), 50.9 million children live in extreme poverty-37.7 million in the villages, 10.2 million in towns and cities and 3 million in tribal areas.

A more recent estimate (April 1977), indicates that as many as 126 million children may be living below the poverty line.

Birth Rate and Mortality

With a baby every one and a half seconds, there are 1.7 million births a month and 21 million births a year in India. Balanced against the annual total death rate of 8 million-which includes 3.2 million infants and children-this means that about 13 million children are added to the country's population every year.

The rural birth rate-35.8 per 1000 population-is much higher than the urban birth rate of 28.3 per 1000 population.

Mortality: The child's fight for survival does not always succeed, and for every 1000 babies born alive, 122 die in the first year of life.

Infant and toddler deaths add up to 2 million in the 0-12 month age group and 1.2 million in the 1-4 year group. Together, these deaths account for 40 per cent of the total annual deaths in the country.

The combined mortality rate for the lowest age group (0-4 years) is three and a half times that of the next age group (5-14 years).

The infant mortality rate has fallen steadily during the century, but remains high.

From 204 per 1000 live births in 1915, and 161 per 1000 live births in 1945, the average national infant mortality rate currently stand at 122 per 1000 live births. However, rural-urban imbalances persist, with the rural rate averaging rate of 81 per 1000 live births. After the first week of life; the infant mortality rate of females is higher than that of males throughout the first year of life.

Life Expectancy: If an Indian child survives the early childhood years, life expectancy for a boy is 53 years and for a girl, 52 years.

Definition

Birth Rate: The number of live births in 1 year per 1,000 population. This will vary with the average age of the population and with the male/female ratio, as well as with other factors.

Infant Mortality Rate: Infants under 1 year of age dying in 1 year, per 1,000 live births. The younger the child at death, and the greater the distance from the registration centre, the less likely it is to be registered either as a birth or death.

Death Rate: The number of deaths registered per 1,000 population. This gives the crude death rate. Deaths may be further analyzed by age, by sex, by occupation, by social class, by diseases, by district, and by various other relevant factors. Death rates by age-groups may be calculated per 1,000 of population or per 1,000 of that age-group.

Health

Children in India face many health hazards, and many die young for lack of timely health care.

Forty per cent of all deaths in India occur among children below 5 years of age. Of these deaths, about half are of children less than a year old.

In the lowest age group (0-12 months), 50 per cent of deaths are due to dysentery, diarrhea, respiratory diseases and gastro-intestinal disorders. In the 1-4 year group, mortality seems to be specifically related to respiratory, digestive and parasitic diseases. These in turn are aggravated by poor environmental sanitation, overcrowded living conditions, and malnutritions. Ignorance of simple health precautions also takes its toll.

It is estimated that 30 per cent of all school-going children are suffering from one or other ailment. Of children's illnesses treated at health centres, 56 per cent respiratory complaints and nutritional disorders. Eye ailments and defects due to poor diet and poor hygiene are also common, and many children needlessly go blind in early childhood. Tuberculosis is widespread in small children.

Health Services: About 80 per cent of Indians live in rural and tribal areas, but only 30 per cent of doctors in the country are available there.

Medical care for the rural population is provided by government-run primary health centres. Each centre is expected to serve from 70,000 to 80,000 people, spread over a hundred villages, with the help of two doctors. Some PHCs have only one doctor. Each PHC auxiliary nurse-midwife serves 10,000 people in 10 to 12 village. The average distance between the village and the health centre is 9 km. and about 87 per cent of people attending the PHCs are from villages within a 6.4 km. radius. Many children do not get timely attention because 50 per cent of village women are daily wage earners, and they cannot carry their small children to the PHC without losing family earning. Under the government's new rural health scheme, villagers trained as community health workers are gradually extending health care to village homes. AT the time of childbirth, few women receive skilled assistance; the proportion ranges from 20 to 50 pre cent in different parts of the country.

The number of hospital beds for children-about 9,300-is barely 50 per cent of the minimum requirement, and the country has only 25 children's hospitals and 424 paediatric wards-to meet the needs of nearly 250 million children. Most of these are located far from the village. There are major regional disparities; Bihar; Gujarat and Haryana do not have any children's hospitals at all.

The existing maternal and child health services reach only a small proportion of the women and children who need them. Women in the 15-45 age group constitute nearly 22 per cent of the population, and children in the 0-6 age group comprise another 21 per cent. Meeting the health needs of this 43 per cent of the population remains a major national task.

Water and Health: Water-borne and water-related diseases are the leading killers of infants and children. About 163 million children (0-14 years) in rural India do not have access to safe drinking water, and are thus exposed to infection which can prove fatal.

In 113,000 village, the drinking water supply is either more than 1.6 km. away, or is substandard, and is responsible for diseases like cholera and guinea-worm, or problems related to a mineral content too high for health.

In another 24,000 village, the water supply from wells, streams, tanks, ponds and rivers, is adequate in quantity, but is open to the risk of pollution.

There are at least 185,000 villages where the supply of

water is both inadequate and unprotected.

It is estimated that about 8.7 per cent of deaths in the first year of life, 19.1 per cent of deaths in the 1-4 age group and 15.2 per cent of deaths in the 5-15 group are due to diarrhea.

Nutrition

Malnutrition is a major cause of death among children in India. Every month 1,00,000 children die from its effects. An even larger number of children die of infectious diseases, their poor diet having made them susceptible to infection and vulnerable thereby to death.

Children survive malnourishment depending on the degree of deficiency. For every child who shows clinical signs of malnutrition, there are probably at least 4 children suffering from milder grades of malnutrition without clinically apparent symptoms. There are an estimated 60 million malnourished children in India.

Approximately 80 to 90 per cent of Indian children do not receive adequate amount of key vitamins and minerals; 75 per cent do not receive adequate calories and about 50 per cent do not receive enough proteins.

Acute diarrhoeal diseases are more frequent and serious among these malnourished children than among those of nutritional status.

Pre-School Children: Some 60 per cent of children in the 0-60 years age group suffer from nutritional anaemia and protein-calorie malnutrition in one form or the other. Almost 40 per cent of all deaths in the country occur in this age group and the majority of these fatal cases are attributed to kwashirokar, Vitamin A deficiency and anaemia. Again three-fourths of the children, 52 per cent suffer from moderate malnutrition, 23 pre cent from severe malnutrition and only 3 per cent can be considered as having normal body weight.

Children from the low socio-economic strata suffer the worst. 80 per cent of them are victims of moderate or severe protein-calorie malnutrition, as shown by their sub-standard body weights.

School-going Children: It is estimated that 22 per cent of the school-going children show one or more signs of nutritional deficiency. The most common are anaemia, higher proportion of school-going children from low socio-economic groups (56 per cent) show signs of moderate protein-calorie malnutrition. While 15 per cent show severe malnutrition, reflected in sub-standard body weights.

Vitamin-A Deficiency: About 2.5 million children in India are threatened by blindness in early childhood because their diet lacks Vitamin A. Severe Vitamin A deficiency is estimated at a million cases. About 12,000 to 14,000 children of the toddler age group go blind every year because of this deficiency. Lack of the vitamin is also behind the night blindness that afflicts about 10-15 per cent of all children.

One out of every four cases of blindness is due to dietary deficiency of Vitamin-A, and is therefore, preventable. The peak incidence of such blindness is in the 1-5 years age group.

Child Nutrition and the Family: Maternal malnutrition is a major contributory factor in the premature birth of an infant. It has been found that 36 pre cent of infant deaths are due to prematurity.

Studies also indicate that when the family size is small, the nutritional level of each child is better, while in larger families, the children born later are more prone to nutritional deficiencies. Research indicates that among the first three children born to a family, only 17 per cent show signs of malnutrition, while among the fourth and younger children 32 per cent had malnutrition symptoms.

Education

A Directive Principle of the Indian Constitution (Article

45) lays down that the State shall endeavor to provide free and compulsory education for all children until they complete 14 years of age. This was to have been achieved within a decade, but has not been realized so far.

The progress has been uneven from state to state, as between the urban and rural areas and as between boys and girls. For example, all urban areas have facilities for elementary and middle school education. In rural areas, 80 per cent of the habitations have a primary school within 1.5 km. and over 60 per cent of the habitations have a middle school within 3 km. out of a total of 575,926 village in the country, it is estimated that about 48,566 are not served by any school at all.

Education is free for all children up to the secondary stage in 12 states and union territories. In 8 other States and union territories, it is free for all children up to the middle school stage. Another 8 states offer free education for all children up to the middle school stage, and up to a few more years only for girls. Two states offer free and one of them offers an additional few years of free education for girls.

School Enrollment: Approximately 4.5 million children are being offered one kind of pre-primary programmes or the other. These from barely 5 per cent of the population in the 3-6 years age group and are mainly from the better-off sections of society.

Enrollment in schools has been slower than expected. Only 80.9 per cent of children in the 6-11 years age group, 37.0 per cent in the 11-14 years age group and 20.9 per cent children in the 14-17 years age group are enrolled in schools. The enrollment level for girls is much lower than that for boys. While the enrollment of boys of the 6-11 years age group is 97.5 pre cent, it is only 63.5 per cent for girls of that group. In the 11-14 years age group, the enrollment of boys is 48.7 per cent, but that of girls is only 24.5 per cent. The gap widens further at the high school level (14-17 years) with enrollment of boys at 28.8 per cent and that of girls at just 12.3 per cent.

Dropout Rates: The school enrollment figures provide only one aspect of children's education, another being the rate of dropping out from school.

Out of every 100 children who enter Class I, less than half complete Class V and only 24 complete Class VIII. The dropout rate for girls is much higher. Of every 200 girls who join Class I, only about 30 reach Class V. Thus, 70 per cent of girls who get enrolled leave school without attaining functional literacy.

Handicapped Children

Four major disabilities affect at least three million children in the country. Estimates list 2 million mentally retarded, 800,000 blind, 500,000 orthopedically handicapped and 200,000 deaf children.

These modest estimates do not include the large number of children who are marginally or mildly handicapped. While about 12,000 to 14,000 children go blind every year due to Vitamin A deficiency, about 10 to 15 pre cent of all children suffer from night blindness. Available data does not give a clear picture of the actual incidence of these and other handicaps.

Services and facilities for the education, training and rehabilitation of handicapped children are grossly inadequate. Existing services cater to only 4 per cent of the physically handicapped, 2 per cent of the blind, 2 per cent of the deaf and barely 0.2 per cent of the known mentally retarded child population. There are only 800 voluntary organizations and State institutions offering educational and training facilities to about 30,000 handicapped children.

Prevailing social attitudes towards mental and physical handicaps are an additional problem for the handicapped child.

The Deprived Child

The Submerged Segment: An estimated 46 per cent of the population live below the poverty line-48 per cent in the rural areas and 41 per cent in the urban areas. This means that approximately 108 million children live in varying degrees of destitution, 90.5 million of them in the village and 17.4 million in the towns.

The Depressed Classes: There is a predictable overlapping of the child population living in poverty and that belonging to the scheduled castes and tribes. The vast majority of children belonging to the scheduled castes and tribes live in an environment that hampers even a minimum development, like urban slums, shanty towns, backward villages, and inaccessible tribal areas.

About 21.5 per cent of the total child population belongs to the scheduled castes and tribes. Among the 33.5 million scheduled caste children, 29.6 million live in years of age. All but 500,000 of the 15.9 million children of scheduled tribes live in rural areas, and 7.7 million of them are under 6 years old.

Destitute and Vagrant Children: The 1971 census listed 151,000 children as beggars or vagrants-120,000 in rural areas and 30,000 in the towns. Of those listed, West Bengal-with 26 per cent of the national total-accounted for the largest number. Uttar Pradesh, Andhra Pradesh, Maharashtra, Karnataka and Orissa have the next largest incidence of beggary, in that order. It is likely that the actual number of children in India pushed into beggary is greater than the census data indicates. Police records show that nearly a third of all beggar children have one or both parents living; the parents themselves use their children for begging. Other children may be victims of cruel exploitation in beggar and mutilated and forced to beg. Their earnings go to the so-called beggar barons.

Throw-away Babies: It is estimated that about a million babies out of the 21 million born every year become 'throw away' babies, abandoned soon after birth due to various social and economic pressures. Social workers estimates place the number of destitute orphaned of the total child population. Only about 25,000 of such children are in the care of some kind of institution. In most orphanages, female children outnumber males, reflecting the greater value placed on sons in Indian society.

Children of Migrants: Migrants are usually unskilled, displaced labourers moving from place to place in search of work. They seldom manage to get more than casual daily wages or short-term seasonal employment. In 1971 families who had been in their place of residence for less than one year. Of these, 3.3 million children were in the rural areas, and 0.9 million in urban areas.

Most migrant families live at subsistence level. They do without protected water supply, without proper housing, sanitation or sewage services, and are often outside the radius of medical and schooling facilities. Migrants children grow up exposed to disease and disability, and deprived of a settled existence. Formal education barely figures in their lives.

Both boys and girls of migrant families take up petty jobs to add to the meager family earnings. An urban study showed that while about 19 per cent of the children of settled city-dwellers were workers, child labour among migrant children was as high as 80 per cent. There is no comparable data available on the labour rate among children of rural migrants.

Poor nutrition low resistance to disease and insanitary conditions combine to undermine the physical status of the migrant child. While the urban infant mortality rate is otherwise 83 per cent 1000 in some urban slums and migrant settlements it is as high as 140 per 1000.

Working Children

Lack of data makes it difficult to arrive at a reliable

figure of the number of children pushed into the labour force by economic pressures. The 1971 census listed 10.7 million children as workers, but estimates indicate that the total child labour force may be as high as 30 million.

it is assumed that 5 to 10 per cent of India's children are working. India has the largest number of child workers in the world. These children constitute about 6 per cent of the total labour force in the country.

Of the 10.7 million children classified as workers in 1971 census data, 7.9 million were boys and 2.8 million girls. This data does not seem to adequately reflect the role of girls in the family-based economy. The proportion of girls, to female adult workers has been found to be about 10 per cent higher than the proportion of boys to male adult workers.

Where They Work: Where do child labourers work? The majority are in agriculture or farm-related work, or in the unorganized sector. Of the 10.7 million listed as child labour in 1971, only those working in the organized sector of the economy are expected to benefit from various child protection laws. Most child workers are outside the scope of such protective legislation. Out of the known figures, about 78.7 per cent work as cultivators and agricultural labourers, and another 8.2 per cent are engaged in livestock raising, forestry, fishing, hunting, plantation and orchard work. About 6 per cent in household and other industries, with the rest engaged in trade, commerce, transport and storage.

The number of children employed in the unorganized sector is not reflected in census data and can only be guessed at. This sector accounts for children working as domestic servants, helpers in hostels, restaurants, canteens, wayside shops and similar establishment; hawkers, newspaper venders, porters, shoe-shine boys, sweepers and scavengers, children employed in small sites engaged in breaking stones, loading and unloading goods. Their working and living conditions bad. They are at the mercy of their employers.

Where They Come From: According to the 1971 data, about 93 per cent of child workers belong to rural areas. They constitute 5.3 per cent of the total rural child population. The 9 per cent of child workers found in urban areas constitute 1.8 per cent of the total urban child population. The 1971 data places the incidence of child labour as highest in Andhra Pradesh, which accounts for 15.2 per cent of India's total child labour force, and 9 per cent of the State's labour force. The next highest recorded incidence is in Madhya Pradesh and Orissa.

Frequent migration seems to encourage early employment of children. Data indicates that as many as 80 per cent of the children of migrants are workers. This is four times higher than the rate among settled populations.

What It Means: Child labour deprives children of educational opportunities, minimizes their chances for vocational training, hampers their intellectual development and by forcing them into the army of unskilled labourers, condemns them to low wages all their wages.

Exploitation: Existing legislation covering child workers in factories and establishments is not being adequately enforced. There are also areas where no legislative coverage exists, and others where the laws themselves permit early childhood employment.

Juvenile Delinquency

Juvenile crime accounts for 3.4 per cent of all cognisable crime in India. Its rate is estimated to be 6.4 per 100,000 population.

Contributing Factors: There seems to be a strong relationship between poverty and the incidence of juvenile crime. It is found that the lower the income of the family, the higher the incidence of juvenile crime. Among the children arrested for crimes under the Indian Penal Code, it was found that 83 per cent belonged to families where the joint income of parents and guardians was less than Rs. 150 per month; 13.4 per cent of families whose income was between Rs. 150 and Rs. 499 per month; 3.12 per cent of families whose income was between Rs. 500 and Rs. 1000 per month and 0.36 per cent of families whose income was above Rs. 1000 per month.

Among the children apprehended, it was found that 48 per cent were illiterate, 34.6 per cent were below the primary level of schooling and 11.5 pre cent were above the primary but below the higher secondary level.

Pattern of Crime: Among the crimes committed by juvenile delinquents are murder, kidnapping, abduction, dacoity, robbery, burglary, theft, riot, criminal breach of trust and cheating. The largest percentage of juvenile crimes fall under the Gambling Act, the Prohibition Act and the Indian Railways Act.

The Spread: About 30 per cent of juvenile crime was reported in Maharashtra, followed by 18 per cent in Gujarat, 16 per cent in Tamil Nadu and 11.5 per cent in Madhya Pradesh.

Among the children apprehended, it was found that 17 per cent had been apprehended for repeated crimes.

Enforcement of Laws: Most of the Children Acts have a clause for providing a 'place of safety' where child offenders can be kept in custody separately from the adult offenders. Despite this, it is estimated that in the various states and union territories of India, there are 10,000 children under 16 years of age confined to prison along with adult offenders.

Existing legislation in most states does not mention anything about the time limit for detention of the child till he is brought before the court. Often, because of this, children are kept in detention of long periods without being brought before a magistrate.

Children in Need of Day-Care

Many of India's children are neglected during early childhood for lack of day-care services. Shortage of such services often pulls an older sister out of school to shoulder the task, or forces a working mother to take small children to work sites, where they face added hazards.

The 1971 census lists 16.6 million rural children and 2 million urban children less than 6 years old, whose mothers are workers. The 1971 data also lists 31 million women workers, of whom about 20 million belong to the most needy sections of society. About 94 per cent of women labourers work in the unorganized sector where employers do not provide any service for their children. Day-care facilities for the children of these working mothers remain a major unmet need.

What the Law Says: The law does provide for day-care services for children of certain categories of women workers, but many employers do not fulfill legal obligations. Women working in the unorganized sector, or provisions. Nor are women as clerks, teachers, nurses, and similar lower-level white collar employees.

Under the Contract Labour Regulations and Abolition Act of 1970, a contractor must provide a creche wherever 20 or more women are employed as contract labour. This is seldom done.

Under the Factories Act (Section 48), every factory ordinarily employing 50 or more women workers has been obliged to provide and maintain creches for children under 6 years old. But this stipulation of the Act is openly violated, and in 1973 there were only 901 factories in the country providing this facilities. With the enforcement of the Factories (Amendment) Act of 1976, the obligation has been extended to every factory employing a minimum of 30 women workers.

The Plantation Labour Act of 1951 stipulates that every plantation employing 50 or more women workers should provide a creche for these workers children. Strict enforcement of these laws is an urgent need. Day-care services are also badly needed by women workers falling outside the scope of these laws.

Legislation

Legislation support for child welfare services in India is found in the Children Acts of the various states. These laws have a special relevance to the protection and rehabilitation of socially handicapped children such as neglected, destitute, victimized, delinquent and exploited children.

The biggest drawback of the Children Acts is that the 'child' is defined differently from state to state. In Madhya Pradesh, Uttar Pradesh and Punjab, a child means a person under 16 years, in Saurashtra and West-Bengal a person under 18 years in Telengana a person under 16 years. In the union territories, a child is defined as a movement of exploited children cannot be prevented, these laws are not as effective as they could have been.

Some states, like Nagaland, Orissa, Sikkim and Tripura, have yet to enact any children's legislation. The union territories of Andaman and Nicobar Islands, Arunchal Pradesh, Chandigarh, Dadra and Nagar Haveli, Lakshdweep and Mizoram have no institutional arrangements yet to apply the Children Act of 1960.

Protecting the Working Child: The main thrust of the Indian laws concerning child labour has been on the minimum age of employment, medical examination of children and prohibition of night work. In each of these directions, the standards stipulated are below the international levels laid down by the international Labour Organization. Enforcement of the law is rendered difficult by a combination of factors: economic backwardness forcing the family to supplement its income by letting the children work; lack of educational facilities: the unorganized nature of a good part of economy; and the smallness of most manufacturing units.

Minimum Age: A major deficiency in the protective legislation is the fact that there is no law fixing a minimum age for employment in agriculture, though it is the main occupation in the country and the bulk of child labour. 78.7 per cent of it, is engaged in this occupation. A plantations. 14 years in factories and 12-14 years in the case of non-industrial employment. But this leaves the small sector unregulated: for example, the Factories Act itself applies only to factories employing workers above a minimum number.

Medical Fitness: As for legal safeguards for the health of child workers, the law require medical examination of children up to 18 years of age and that too for industrial employment only. But no standards are laid down for medical fitness. And there is no law in respect of medical examination of children working in the non-industrial sector.

Adoption of Children: The Adoption of Children Bill was introduced in Parliament in 1972, but has yet to be enacted. Its aim is to provide an enabling law for all Indians seeking to adopt the many abandoned, destitute, neglected and orphaned children in the country. This was in pursuance of the directive principle in the constitution of preventing the moral and material abandonment of children (Article 39f).

The existing Hindu Adoption and Maintenance Act covers only that community.

Child Marriage: Throughout the 50 years of its existence, the Sharda Act (The Child Marriage Restraint Act) has been an ineffective legislative showpiece. Although it was meant to prohibit child marriage altogether, the question of validity of a child marriage solemnized in violation of the statutory age requirements remained outside its scope.

The Child Marriage Restraint Amendment Act, 1978 raises the minimum age of marriage from 18 to 21 years for boys and 15 to 18 years for girls. Even with this amendment, the violation of the law would not affect the only entail penal consequences. Offenses under the Sharda Act have now become cognisable and even Muslim, Parsi and Jewish communities come within its purview even though it does not affect their personal laws. Parental consent no longer exempts a child marriage from the provisions of the amended law. This was a loophole in the original law.

Experience shows that legal changes may not cause marriages to be delayed, unless constructive opportunities are provided to the young persons whose marriage are sought to be postponed till the legally permissible age.

5

Welfare Programmes for Child Development

Introduction

After Independence, the government of free India initiated planned efforts for development of rural India and for the socio-economic growth of the rural poor/weaker sections. Since then, although there have been programmatic changes and shifts, in emphasis, the effort has been on, and considerable amounts of the country's scarce resources were being set and geared to year after year for achieving the objective. But in view of the giganticity of the task, and the thin spread of the benefits that have resulted from the efforts so far put in, we have still a long way to travel in order to see that the little communities living in our vast rural areas transformed into productivity and forward-looking vibrant communities.

Rural development being multi-disciplinary in nature and multisectoral in operation, is designated to fulfill multiple objectives, namely more production, more employment and more equitable distribution of income, wider participation in the development process, increased access to modern inputs and services and greater self-reliance and environmental awareness.

Of later, several contradictions have arisen as various components of rural development plans and programmes have been ill concerned, fragmented and sometimes, almost unrelated. As a result, the question of rural development in recent years have loomed large and is being discusses, more with concern and attention than casual romantic euphoria, at the various national and international forums of academics, intellectuals, administrators, politicians and planners etc.

Since last four decades, the rural development in India has witnessed Kaleidoscopic changes from time to time. In this context various programmes were introduced under different names, starting from Community Development (CD) to Integrated Rural Development Programme (IRDP) although their contents remains almost the same and also the fate of the people marked no substantial change. However,different approaches to rural development adopted during plan periods can broadly be grouped as:

Community Development Approach

-- Launched in 1952
-- Culminated in Panchayat Raj structure in 1955

Growth Centre Approach

-- Radiate employment,income boosting projects
-- Reinforcing relationship between core and periphery

Sectoral Approach

- Intensive sectoral deveiopment like-agriculture industry etc.

Target Sector Approach

-- IRDP,MNP,SMFDP and package programme (Green Revolution launched)

Pilot Project Approach

-- Pilot project evolved to assist small and marginal farmers as such SFDA & MFDA programmes launched

I.R.D. Approach

-- Latest approach

-- Integrated development

-- Inter-relation between different activities.

From this perspective the Indian rural development programmes have been reformist in nature. Here, instead of directly going to the root cause of rural poverty and hunger, so as to alleviate them, under the influence of Gandhism a reformist line was adopted which deterred and diverted the radical outlook.

However,as rural development is characterized by a combination of both an applied and theoretical aspects and the scope is primarily restricted to rural sector and encompassed all facets of rural life, it is subject-matter necessitates an appropriate understanding in spheres which are closely related to the development of the lives of the people. Further, it does not depend only on the promotion of social and economic activities but also on such other inputs which have close bearing on the lives of people such as health,nutrition, education and skill development.

During the past four decades of plan development,social welfare as a plan component has acquired great significance, as evidenced by its widening interface with government and increasing participation by voluntary agencies. From the Fifth

Plan onwards, emphasis has been on the promotion of preventive and developmental services. As a result several programmes in the areas of child welfare viz. nutrition, health, education and recreation for children have launched by the Government. Plan-wise rural development programme, its objective, year of introduction etc.related to women and children.

So far as child welfare is concerned, as a concept and practice it has deep historical roots in our country. In their earlier days as stated by Chowdhry (1984)'Child Care Services were confined to the voluntary sector. These services were mainly organized for victims of destitution, delinquency, abuse etc. In mid-twenties, voluntary organization such as Indian Council for Child Welfare, the Indian Red Cross Society, the All India Women's Conference, the Kasturba Gandhi National Memorial Trust, the Bankanji Bari, the Children's Aid Society etc. organized programmes in the areas of care, health nutritional and education for children etc.

The status of child indicates that children's programmes need the highest priority in the national development programmes. Earlier, child care had been the responsibility of the primary institutions of the society such as family and in most of the cases, the joint family. The child's physical, psychological, social and cognitive development was assured by the resources and the surrounding of the joint family. The transition from joint to nuclear family and changes in socio-economic status have brought many changes in society. Because of the new constraints,traditional care suffered progressive erosions. Child neglect,abuse and exploitation followed. As a large number of families, both in rural and urban areas are below poverty line, these sections of the population are even today not in a position to provide the care and security needed for normal growth of their children. Intervention by the government therefore, becomes imperative for their proper health care,nutrition, education and well-being. It is in this view, the subject, at the same time, also requires a clear understanding of the planning process and the different rural development programmes which are being envisaged for the welfare of children from time to time for the welfare of children from time to time.

After realizing the significance of child development an attempt has been made in the present exercise to give a critical review of the programmes meant for this vulnerable group. The focus is primarily on rural development programmes only. The paper is split into five parts including the present one. The second part gives a brief sketch of child development during plan period. The third takes the vivid account of child development programmes whereas fourth examines the programmes critically. The final part offers a closing statement by highlighting same issues.

II. Child Development during Five Year Plans

In the First Five Year Plan, the major responsibility of developing children's welfare service was placed on voluntary organizations; states too assumed greater responsibility and launched programmes for health, nutrition and primary education of children. Pre-primary education, however,continued to be the responsibility of voluntary organizations. The Second Five Year Plan reiterated that voluntary efforts in child welfare have to be supplemented by central, state and local authorities. The Central Social Welfare Board (CSWB) was given the responsibility of promoting and developing welfare services for women and children in the voluntary sector through grants-in-aids programmes. Welfare Extension Project programmes was expanded and coordinated with similar programmes of the Ministry of Community Development of women and children in community development blocks.

In order to combat rural malnutrition, Applied Nutrition Programme was started during Third Five Year Plan with the assistance of UNICEF, FAO and WHO. This was followed by supplementary Nutrition Programme in 1970-71 by the

Ministry of Social Welfare. Balwadi Nutrition Programme funded by the Government was also introduced in the same year. However, there was no scheme for universal courage of the rural pre-school children till the Fourth Five Year Plan.

In spite of launching a number of child welfare programmes, the incidents of mortality, morbidity and malnutrition among children continued to be alarmingly high. A national Policy for Children was formulated followed by the setting-up a National Children's Board. The Ministry of Social Welfare developed the Integrated Child Development Service Schemes (ICDS) in 1975 and 33 project of (ICDS) were launched on an experimental basis in 1975-76.

The Ministry of Rural Development has also introduced a scheme of Development of Women and Children in Rural Areas (DWCRA) as a part of the Integrated Rural Development Programmes during Sixth Five Year Plan. During Seventh Five Year Plan the wheat-based Nutrition Programmes was launched in 1986 by the Department of Women and Child Development.

However,after reviewing the programmes launched during different periods, we can examine the trends of the programmes in the past and in the current decade.

Thinking Trends of the Planners/Policy-Makers

Before		Now
Social Welfare Oriented	-	Development Oriented.
Child Development as some responsibilities	-	Accept the children as human resources develop ment in and needs different socioeco nomic set-up
Children's programme isolated from the main stress	-	Integration in the major programme for over all development.

Oriented to the delivery of services - Participatory in nature.

However,much ground needs to be covered yet to achieve the goal by way of creating an atmosphere of better understanding of the development needs for children in the context of national developmental strategy and a strong infrastructure and other supports to achieve the goal.

III. Rural Development Programmes in the Context of Child Development

In the early fifties, development of programmes for women, children and youth in the rural areas was the responsibility of the Ministry of Community Development. However, because of limited resources in the community development budget, the social factors in rural development did not get due importance in community development in subsequent Five Year Plans. Children did not get as much attention as they needed nor did they get as much share of the increased income as they should have for this growth and development.

As a result, to cover this gap, different ministries of the government launched various programmes which aimed at raising the quality of life particularly of women and children. Broadly speaking the different rural development programmes related to children can be grouped as,

(a) health;
(b) nutrition;
(c) education; and
(d) integration of different services.

Details of the programmes are given in the subsequent paragraphs.

Health Related Programmes

The situation of Children in India is far from satisfaction with no access to proper food, shelter or sanitary facilities.

Though most of the child health components are covered by Child Development Programme, MNP and ICDS and very few are left like immunization, MCH and programme for some preventive measures. Some of these programmes are summarized here.

Immunization Programme: Public Health Programme in India has been operating at two planes. At one plane, an integrated curative and public health services are provided through the PHCs under the Health Department. At another plane big national programmes have been developed to tackle diseases like Malaria, Small Pox, Tuberculosis, Leprosy, Filariasis and Trachoma. An Expanded Programme of Immunization (EPI) has also been adopted for providing protection against Tetanus, Diphtheria, Whooping cough, Poliomyalitis and Tuberculosis. The programmes emerge at the initiative of the Central Government, and are executed at the States. The expenditure on these programmes is also borne wholly or largely by the Central Government. These constitute,so to say, the Central Contribution to the health services for the nation.

MCH Programme : In India, primary health centres are the backbone of rural services. Within limited resources, primary health care is probably the best available alternate for providing MCH services in rural areas.

One of the factors which has a direct bearing on the rate of mortality is the type of medical attention received at birth. In rural areas over 75 per cent births are attended by untrained medical practitioners or others and only about 8 per cent by trained medical practitioners. However, with introduction of the latest scheme of providing at least one trained dia (Traditional Birth Attendant Programme) in each village is hoped that there will improvement in this situation.

CHV/VHG/CHW Programme : The Community Health Workers or Village Health Guide Scheme is a step towards taking health services to the actual needy groups. Under this scheme an attempt in being made to make health services available to villagers at their doorstep.

(b) Nutritional Related Programmes

Several nutrition programmes are in operation in order to combat the problem of malnutrition. Most of them are short-term measures to supplement the diets of pre-school children,pregnant and lactating mothers. Some important among these are summarized here.

Applied Nutrition Programme (ANP): The Expanded Nutrition Programme (1959) was renamed as Applied Nutrition Programme and aimed at extending the services to the rural areas. Feeding, however, was limited to the vulnerable group i.e.children in the age groups of 0-6 years and pregnant and nursing mothers. Drought-prone and backward area were given priority over the others. It was implemented through C.D. blocks. Organization of poultry units, horticulture, kitchen gardens, community gardens were the methods of production of food with the intention of bringing about greater awareness with regard to the production and consumption of protective foods. The feeding component was limited only to the use of food produced by vulnerable groups and was basically as a farm of practical demonstration for the beneficiaries.

Intensive Development Programme (IDP): An IDP (1977-78) consisted of a package of inter-related basic services which could be delivered to specifically identified rural areas in order to improve the health and nutritional status of young children and their mothers. According, 23 on-going ANP blocks in 21 States were selected for intensive development with the UNICEF assistance for a period of two years. The programmes under this experiment covered, in addition to ANP activities, safe drinking water, environmental sanitation, income generating activities for women etc.

Special Nutrition Programme (SNP): This programme was launched as a crash feeding programme in 1970-71 to provide supplementary feeding to children below 6 years and expectant and nursing mothers living in urban slums, tribal,backward and rural areas and aims at bridging the existing nutritional gap in the target groups by providing supplementary feeding to the extent of 200 calories and 10-12 grams of protein for 300 days a year. Later on (during 5th Plan 1974-78), it was transferred to the state sector to be operated as a part of the Minimum Needs Programme with a special officer in-charge of the programme under the Director of Social Welfare at the State level.

Balwadi Nutrition Programme (BNP)(1970-71): Children in the age group of 3-6 years from low income families of the rural areas are the main target groups of the BNP. It provides educational facilities for pre-school children and nutritional supplement to pre-schoolers with intention of elevating their nutritional status.

Mid-day Meal Programme (MDM) : It was initiated in 1962-63 as a centrally sponsored scheme and later on transferred to MNP. Attempt is being made under this programme to offer a free meal to school-going children between 6-11 years from the weaker sections of society. The programme provides one meal containing about 80 grams of food grains and 7 grams of oil with a nutritive content of approximately 300 calories and 8-12 grams protein for a period of at least 180 days in a years per beneficiary.

Vitamin A Prophylaxis Programme : This programme was launched by the Ministry of Health and Family Welfare in 1970. The programme aims at reducing incidence of blindness occurring due to deficiency of Vitamin A. Children in the age-group of 1-5 years from the target group and 200,000 1.U. of Vitamin A suspension in oil is provided to all the beneficiaries once every six months.

Prophylaxis Against Nutritional Anaemia (PANA) : In order to meet deficiency of hemoglobin level in pre-school children and pregnant women at later stages of pregnancy, the Ministry of Health and Family Welfare launched this programme. Iron and folic acid supplements to the extent of 60 mg. of iron as ferrous sulphate or ferrous furmamrate and 0.5 mg.folic acid are provided to expectant mothers and 20 mg.iron and 0.1 mg.folic acid are given to pre-school children for approximately 100 days consecutively.

(c) Education Related Programmes

A number of Committees and study groups were set-up from time to time suggest ways and means for pre-school education families. All these groups emphasized the importance of pre-school education but the recommendations remained mostly on paper. The CSWB initiated as a part of its welfare activities in the areas not covered hitherto, the scheme of Welfare Extension Projects. But most of the children education programmes are integrated with the health and nutritional programme. However, a great impetus to the provision of pre-school education was provided by the declaration of a National Policy on Children in 1974 which recognized children as the supreme asset of the nation. This was followed by the launching of Integrated Child Development Service Scheme.

(d) Integrated Programmes

Since the Fourth Five Year Plan integration of different services specially in the rural sector was started. At the out set Minimum Need Programme was first among the different programmes.

Minimum Need Programme(MNP): This programme was launched in 1972 with an objective to develop basic infrastructural facilities and to increase health and nutritional status of children and nursing mothers. It consists of the following elements:

(i) Elementary Education: 100 per coverage of children

in the age group of 6-14 years.

(ii) Adult Education: Establishment of PHC/Sub-centre and one CHV/VHG in each village.

(iii) Rural Health: Coverage of all problem villages.

(iv) Rural Water Supply: Coverage of all problem villages.

(v) Rural Roads: linking of all villages with a popu lation of 1000 or more;

(vi) Rural Electrification: Coverage of 60 per cent villages in each State.

(vii) House-sites for landless: Provision of housing assistance to all rural landless labourers.

(viii) Nutrition: SNP to malnourished children, pregnant and lactating mothers, supplementary feeding to pre-school children for 300 days.

MDM : Mid-day Meals one-fourth of children in the group 6-11 years to be served in schools for 200 days.

Out of eight components mentioned above only two components viz.elementary education and nutrition are directly related with child development.

Integrated Child Development Services (ICDS)

The earlier efforts made to provide services to the pre-school child were sectoral and lacked necessary coordination. It was feit that a programme may be evolved which was low in cost, economically more comprehensive and effective. As a result, the ICDS scheme was launched in 1975-76 after a series of inter-ministerial discussions.The scheme provides integrated services to:

(a) children below the age of 6 years.

(b) the expectant and nursing mothers, and

(c) Women in the age-group of 15-45.

The following package of services is provided on an integrated basis in the ICDS scheme:

(i) Supplementary nutrition;

(ii) Immunization;

(iii) Health check-up;

(iv) Referral Services;

(v) Nutrition and health education;and

(vi) Non-formal education. The focal point for delivery of these services is the anganwadi centres.

The essence of the programme is 'integration', and is the first major child development programme in the country which has recognized the differential needs of the children 0-6 years age group. The services complementary to one another are integrated into a package to enhance the overall effect. The organization is also integrated through coordination at various levels in the management of services by different departments/agencies running the programme which is inter-sectoral. The blueprint is well-drawn in terms of target groups, services, management, training and funding, the role of different functionaries, monitoring and evaluation.

Development of Women and Children in Rural Areas (DWCRA)

It is a sub-scheme under IRD programme and is introduced on the realization that income of the family is not merely dependent upon the economic programmes but has positive relationship with social inputs.services i.e. nutritional status of family, education, status of women etc. It has drawn the attention on the needs of Rural women and has helped them to take up income generating activities and thereby look after their children better. Besides organizing economic programme, emphasis in training will be given on organization and management of child welfare services. Under this scheme, if the child care services are not available in the area under any other on-going programmes, it will be necessary to provide some facilities so that the children are not neglected while the mothers are at work. Another component of the programme is the provision of certain basic facilities for the care of children at NREP (now JRY) work sites. A provision of Rs. 5000 therefore, has been made for each block for creating temporary child care facilities at the work sits. The programme is being implemented by DRDAs through block functionaries. the districts are selected in consultation with the State Government on the criteria backwards,incidence of child mortality, level of literacy,etc.

A Critical Review

The programme envisaged under community development had a strong component for women and child development,social education etc. But emphasis was more on community development. Even during First, Second, Third and Fourth Five Year Plans programmes for children did not receive any fresh impetus and continued on the earlier lines and were confined to voluntary sector. But after Fourth Plan, Rural Development Programmes for Children received high priority. In the present section we will critically examine the above mentioned programme launched for child development in the subsequent paragraphs.

The PHCs are conceived as focal points from which primary health care services could be provided through dispensaries and sub-centres. The operational responsibilities include medical care, control of communicable diseases, MCH,environmental sanitation, school health, health education, immunization etc. But it is observed that because of lack of proper coordination the above mentioned services of different child health programmes are being ignored by the medical staff. Some of the services like; immunization, school health etc. mentioned above are to be provided at the Anganwadi Centres and schools. But the health functionaries are not performing these responsibilities regularly and hence, it requires proper evaluation.

So far as the nutritional programmes are concerned, various reports and studies reveal that programmes have not succeeded to the extent desired in terms of improvement of dietary pattern and increase in production of protective foods. Poultry and fishery units.(AMP) have failed to make any appreciable impact. Community, school and kitchen gardens had not been develop as they were envisages in the scheme. Use of mass media and other means of communication for nutrition education is marginal. On the basis of these, it has been suggested that nutritional programme should be operated as a part of an overall rural development programme rather than as an independent one.

Involvement of local bodies viz. panchayati raj institutions, mahila mandals and other organization in any of the programme in the promotion is observed to be very unsatisfactory as it was observed by Programme Evaluation Organization (PEO) of Planning Commission.

It has been observed that some of the programmes, services and inputs meant specifically for the children of weaker sections are utilized for the benefit of better-off sections because of weak delivery system. Supplies and services in PHCs or nutrition component of MNP in rural areas go to really a few selected families who are known to the officials. Because of inadequacy of services and delivery system these services do not reach to the needy children. Despite of our efforts for raising the level of children, the rural development programme do not bring results in proportion to which money is spent and efforts are made.

Among the different rural child development programmes, ICDS is single comprehensive and selective on clientele and therefore, economic programme. The services complementary to one another are integrated into a package to enhance the overall effect. The earlier programmes for pre-school children took it for granted that if a balwadi was started, related health and nutrition services will be forthcoming from the other agencies like the PHC and ANP, but the ICDS

Schemes ensures through the budget provisions the necessary direct inputs of health by strengthening and staffing pattern of the PHC,mechanism of proper coordination between health personnel and child development personnel, and organization of training an orientation for these functionaries.

Despite the fact that the programme has many plus points, it has some weaknesses also. One is not so sure whether the children in the age-group of 0-3 years do get the same attention as anganwadi children (3-6 years) in absence of any institution for them. In many project areas, the expected coordination and cooperation from the health staff or the block staff is not forthcoming for various reasons. Institutions have to be created and mechanisms have to be found by which the richer sections should pay for the services be contributing in cash and kind whereas the poorest sections could contribute in the form of voluntary service.

As far as DWCRA programme is concerned,some provision may be made out of its fund for the purchase of portable cradles,toys, pictorial books etc. for the pre-school children. These services can be organized with the help of the community organizer and the gram sevikas.

The community organizer while being trained will also be familiarized with various other ongoing programmes supportive to the development of rural women and children so that the can help in coordinating these activities.

Role of NGO in Child Welfare

I am the child,
All the world waits for my coming
All the earth watches with interest to see what
I shall become
Civilization hangs in balance
For what I am, the world of tomorrow may be
I am the child,
You hold in your hand my destiny
You determine, largely, whether I shall succeed or fail,

Give me, I pray, these things that make for happiness
Train me, I beg you, that
I may be a blessing to the world"
--- Mamie Gene Cole

It is human instinct to protect and care for children out only of one's own but also of others. The children of a country are its valuable asset. No nation on this globe can ignore the responsibility to ensure the proper growth and development of children as the future of the country lies with them. However, as a voiceless section of the society, the children have suffered throughout the ages at the hands of those who are suppose to provide them with security and love. It is not uncommon to find children who have been subjected to abuse, torture or exploitation and who are denied their basic rights. Children are the worst sufferers of wars, natural disasters, unemployment, poverty etc.

The fact that the children are physically and mentally immature necessitates ensuring special rights for their nurture, protection and fulfillments of unique needs. The rights of the child should be a matter of the most vulnerable sections of the society. A deprived child may belong to any religious, ethnic, linguistic, socio-economic category and hence universal acceptance and promotion of child rights needs greater emphasis than the rights of other deprived sections of the society. Such concern crosses national barriers though every nation has to engage itself first in putting its own house in order so that their children are looked after as they ought to.

India having ratified the UN Convention on the Rights of the Child two years ago, is now required to report to the UN Committee on the Rights of the Child, on progress in implementing; the provisions of the convention.

The Convention on the Rights of the Child is unique in the response it has met. No other human rights treaty has been ratified so early by so many. The text was agreed by the UN General Assembly in November 1989. At the end of 1990 no less 57 states had ratified or acceded it and one year later 45 other states had followed.

At the end of 1992 the total number of states Parties had grown to 117- and continued to grow thereafter. Unicef has called for universal ratification by the year 1995. The World Summit for Children in September 1990 has contributed to building this international momentums for the rights of the child.

As a consequence, concrete steps have been taken in various countries to improve the status of children. Legal changes have been made and ;ministrative structures created for the protection of the rights of the child. National Programmes of Action have been written and budgets reviewed in the same spirit. This, however, is only the beginning.

The Convention has created a favorable climate for reform. It has defined universal principles and norms for the status of children. It has, also outlined a process for monitoring and discussing the degree of implementation. Therefore, the Convention can be an instrument for charge and of help of the child rights movement. A details list of countries and their ratification, accession or succession is given at Annexure I.

India has a large number of NGOs, activists and autonomous groups working with children in various parts of the country and range of issues they have taken up covers all the rights enshrined in the Convention. Their involvement in preparation of the country report ensures that it accurately reflects ground realities, and incorporates a critical focus on the progress made in translating policies and programmes into action at the grassroots.

From the outset, Government of India had declared its commitment to an open and consultative process of preparation of the country report. It was agreed that UNICEF would facilitate the NGO input into the country report, in partnership with the Indian Council for Child Welfare, itself a national level child centered NGO in the country. A three-phase process was set up.

* A series of discussion papers around the major themes of the Convention were prepared by individuals or small groups, each with experience and expertise in the particular area.

* These papers were then discussed, critiqued and fleshed out by working groups of experienced and concerned NGO representative, activists, academics and professional at a three-day National Consultation Workshop.

* The outcomes of the consultation were collated by an editorial team to produce the final document, which represents the NGO input into the Government of India report.

Far from being an exercise in self-congratulation, this document incorporates a critical analysis of the legislative, programmatic and administrative frameworks which have been set up to address issues of children's rights. No attempt has been made to enforce conformity with any predetermined formats, and the chapters vary widely in lengths, approach and content. In the case of issues such as alternative care, adoption or leisure and culture, there was a much greater focus on existing programmes and what is being done. In some working groups, the structure of the discussion paper provided the basic outline of the chapter, while in others, discussions resulted in extensive restructuring.

The range, variety and richness of grassroots experiences which enriched the National Consultation cannot, perhaps, be completely or accurately mirrored by any document. However, it is hoped that this report will stand as an expression of the opinions and concerns of NGO, autonomous groups and individuals who share a common commitment to the cause of children's rights.

NGOs and the Welfare of Human Being

1. NGOs fulfill several functions in the field of human rights;

2. Monitoring and fact-finding in their own or other countries;

3. Investigating and reporting on violations;

4. Informing and educating about human rights matters and the work of International Organizations;

5. Mobilizing interest groups and lobbying National Governments and International Bodies;

6. Advising on or directly contributing to the implementation of Human Rights standards.

Which of these functions if performed and how vary from country to country and from NGO to NGO. For instance, some organizations emphasize fact-finding and advocacy, while others give direct service. Naturally, National and International Groups lend to play different, but often complementary roles.

The convention on the Rights of the Child is the only human rights treaty which specifically gives NGOs role in the monitoring procedures. As "other competent bodies" they can be invited by the Committee on the Rights of the Child to give "expert advice". In fact, the Committee has given the NGOs an important place its procedures as given below. It is clear that NGO input will be important for the Committee proceedings.

However, NGOs are important not only in relation to the Committee reporting process. Especially on the National level, they can play a major role increasing awareness about the Convention, its content and mechanisms. They can pressure for ratification and the first legal and administrative steps towards implementation. They can request and contribute to a national systems of monitoring. Finally, they can advocate and/ or undertake themselves the necessary measures to make reality of the standards of the Convention.

For NGOs to be able to take on such tasks their integrity must be respected by the authorities, the NGOs should enjoy the freedom of associating the United Nations should establish this crucial principle. A strong UN position is needed in defense of people and groups working for human rights. The work on a declaration on human rights defenders should be given positive priority. It is an essential task for safe NGOs to support those under threat, in trouble or not even able to establish themselves.

For local and national NGOs to be able to create awareness and inform the public about the Convention of the Rights of the Child, they need themselves information on how the International system works. The International NGOs could play a role on this, but the United Nations should provide basic information on the Convention and its procedures in relevant languages. Interchange between the national and international level is crucial.

India's accession to the UN Convention on the Rights of the Child in December 1992, was an important step towards initiating accountability and reinforcement of the Indian State's commitment towards the survival, protection and development of its children. As outlined of Article 43 of the Convention, all State parties who are signatories to the Convention are obliged to present a report to the Committee on the Rights of the Child for "the purpose of examining the progress made by State Parties in achieving the realization of the obligations undertaken in the present Convention".

The Indian Government is expected to submit its report on the measures they have adopted which give effect to the rights outlined in the Convention to the Committee on the Rights of the Child in Geneva in January 1995. This report is of crucial importance as it will reflect the situation of children in India vis-a-vis their access to rights that the international community has recognized as being crucial to their development and that assures a childhood in conditions of freedom and dignity.

Role of NGOs

Non-Government Organizations, working with children have been the great source of relief especially to the deprived children who live in exceptionally difficult circumstances.

NGOs have made untiring efforts to provide for the basic necessities of life to hitherto most vulnerable group not only through custodial care and protection but also through their developmental approach and participation in policy-making. Looking at the magnitude of the problem, NGOs, however sincere and committed may be their efforts, have not yet been able to reach all the needy children. The reasons are manifold: scarce resources, inadequate trained manpower, lack of co-operation from government and other bodies etc. However in the light of the UN convention on the rights of child, NGOs do have to play greater role at different levels. In the present scenario, this would require redefining their roles, change in approach and global thinking. Acknowledging the fact that NGOs, especially working in the field of human rights, have exercised their influence on the content of convention, the implementation of the same can hardly be effective in absence of participation of voluntary sector in the observance of the provisions of the UN convention.

Approach would be to cater to the different clientele or providing different services to the same clientele in a geographical area. This would require local networking through promotion of joint forums. A remarkable example in this regard is the Forum for Disability formed by NGOs working with disabled in Baroda. In respect of NGOs working with children or having children as one the clientele, such forum will avoid problems of overlapping of its services.

Apart from this, NGOs will have to be prepared for increased participation in regional/local planning bodies as well as policy formulation with regard to the children. The NGOs, besides being supportive, can also take up advocacy and lobbying for children's rights, particularly at such places where there are increased violations of such rights. Not many NGOs have taken up this as one of the key functional areas. If NGOs are able to pose a united front, they would emerge as a potent force for the several initiatives in the area of child welfare and development.

Need for Global Thinking

"Think Globally and Act Locally" has been a popular slogan by now. The problems of children cuts across the boundaries of region, nation and caste, creed as colour. Although the magnitude as well as nature of the problems may vary from one region to the other and from one country to the other, there exists some commonality either in philosophy or future vision. By the end of 1993, 159 countries had either signed the convention or had become state parties to it by ratification. The NGOs of these countries can interact with greater frequency through international bodies like UNICEF and share their experiences, collaborate with each other on the areas common concern, transfer the expertise available ;with one to another and thus make the world better place to live for children. The NGOs at present, no doubt, interact internationally at the initiative of international agencies, frequency of such interaction with emphasis of collaborative approach can increase.

The specific areas where NGOs have to intensify efforts also needs some attention. The UN Convention on the Rights of the Child draws attention to four sets of civil, political, social, economic and cultural rights of every child. These are in the form of the right to survival, the right to protection, the right to development and the right to participation. The key priority areas for NGOs in respect of each of these are discussed below.

1. The Right to Survival

The first and foremost issue that NGOs have to address is disparity in the ratio between boys and girls. According to "The Right to be a Child", a UNICEF India background Paper there are nearly 4 million "missing girls" in the age-group of 0 to 6 years which is a clear indication of female infanticide is the cause for such adverse sex ratio. Along with this, the problem of avoidable child deaths i.e. high infant mortality rate also deserves immediate attention. The present rate of Infant Mortality at 79 and the under five mortality rate of 124 per 1000 births shows a high prevalence of child deaths due to preventable and environmental causes.

It is an established fact that parental education particularly of women and availability as well as utilization of health services would bring about remarkable changes in IMR and increase chances of children surviving to a great extent. NGOs can focus attention on the above two areas. Better provision of health care services can be ensured through active participation of NGOs in health care delivery system, particularly preventive health care, especially in the areas where child survival rate is low.

2. The Right to Development

Although provision of primary education has been the responsibility of the state. Article 45 of The Directive Principles of State Policy as well as the National Policy on Education reflect the firm commitment on the part of state to universalization of free primary education. There is substantial evidence stating progress in the provisioning of primary education in terms of increase in number of primary schools, school teachers, enrollment but there is paucity of reliable date on quality of education and attendance.

The role of NGOs in this regard would undoubtedly centre around providing supportive services as a result of which:

(a) girls can avail the same opportunities that is available to boys;

(b) the drop-out rate is reduced particularly among the disadvantaged sections of the society

(c) assistance to government machinery in better allocation of resources and

(d) help in making education a meaningful experience to the children.

3. The Right to Protection

The right to protection implies prevention of exploitation, abuse and torture which may endanger child's education, health, developmental or survival. India has the long history of economic exploitation of children who are employed as labourer. Poverty and lack of legislative measures to make primary education compulsory drive the children out of school to work in conditions most unfavorable to their growth and development.

The role of NGOs would therefore be to create awareness among masses against the evils of child labour. Moreover, such awareness should be aimed at building public opinion for elimination of child labour. The crucial task for NGOs therefore would be lobbying and advocacy against exploitation and abuse of children in varied form.

4. The Right to Participation

The right to participation includes in it the right of accused children to be treated in just and humane manner. Although a very limited information on juvenile crime is available and the treatment meted out to this children, there is, urgency of action in respect of inevitability of adequate resources to provide for legal representation of accused juveniles, facilities for separate custodial care, rehabilitation services etc. The issue of child marriage is also on forefront which demands intervention by NGOs.

The NGOs can work on the core areas by playing the role of educator as well as activist. In order to ensure fair treatment to the children under custodial care, the NGOs may bridge the gap that exists between general public and children under custodial care which would make worthwhile difference not only on terms of nature of care provided but also safeguard interests of the children. With regard to child marriage, NGOs working in the areas where prevalence rate is higher can take up the issues through public participation in eradication of such evil, seeking co-operation of judicial and executive machinery.

Thus, NGOs have vital role to play with regard to basic and just rights of children. No country shall be able to achieve fulfillment of rights of children without active participation and co-operation from NGOs. The need therefore is to delineate the scope of NGOs functioning and making co-ordinated and concerted efforts towards ensuring children a bright future.

The problem is infact a paucity of lobbyists for child rights and if voluntary organizations and their representatives begin to work as lobbyists for child rights within the nation, there is bound to be more satisfactory input or legislation on child rights.

Voluntary organization can and should ill-afford to be averse to legislation relating to child. They have to first acquaint themselves with the whole gamut of legislative and requirements or the child. They have to strive for achieving and actualizing the legislative goals with the authorities and the law makers with dogged pursuit, wake up those who are insensitive, provide materials in the form of preliminary legislative manuscript and generate a public climate on the urgency of implementing the Convention.

For instance, there could be a comprehensive legislation on child rights which could cover all the diverse aspects of protection and care of the children. Whatever all there is, it is scattered in several statutory enactments covering child rights marginally and the general law is otherwise applied to children, wherever feasible. There is no public library where one could walk in and ask for a walk or material covering all child rights. We are still confounded as to what should be taken as the age of the child in different legislations if existing statutes were to be pursued. There have been cases where a magistrate never verified the age of a child and the Supreme Court had to direct a State Government to enact a law on juvenile justice which it ought to have done 20 years ago. Legislative proposals initiated with great gusto are abandoned or shelved in the absence of crusading lobbyist. It there has been a law in some states no rules were made to implement the law.

Voluntary organization can consider pursuing a CHILD LAWS BILL to provide for the following provisions which the convention envisages but which are not covered by existing Indian Legislation.

1. There has to be uniformity in the definition of 'child' in the context of all legislation.

2. There has to be incorporation or the concept of 'best interests of the child' in Indian law

3. Law has to provide for ensuring the survival rights of the child and this cannot be done unless there is an exclusive law for the child.

4. The right to be cared for by the parents has to be incorporated in the Indian law to curb cases of parental negligence and hard headiness.

5. A child's identity covering abandoned children and of single parents in an evolving Indian society is a must.

6. Children of separated parents should have protection of the law.

7. Special provisions should be made in respect of children used in international entertainments.

8. Though the Indian child is not as matured as his Western counterpart, his views have to be respected through legal provisions.

9. Indian law normally puts responsibility for the child on the father, but both parents must share this responsibility.

10. Children who are mentally and physically disabled have rights no less than normal children and their rights have to be recognized.

11. There has to be a law governing adoption of children.

12. Law must provide for discipline in schools.

NGOs can work individually and in collaboration in some of the following areas.

1. To disseminate information of the Convention of the Rights of the Child through poster, booklets, TV spots, radio jingles, folk art etc., to children, parents, school teachers, functionaries of child care institutions, police, judiciary, employers, Members of Parliament and the general public.

2. To agree/commit one self to help in the gathering of relevant data on status of children vis-a-vis the violation of fundamental rights to survival, protection, growth, development, participation and freedom of expression.

3. To encourage and facilitate the empowerment of children.

4. Take steps to enhance the capacity of NGOs to undertake research, data collection, and analysis on child related subjects so as to come to a better understanding of the various issues and thereby help in formulating relevant and realistic policies and programmes for the protection of Child Rights.

5. To encourage and initiate children into research and data collection on issues relating to them and to enhance their sensitivity to their rights.

6. To take action-legal or through mass protest against any violation of a child's rights. As NGOs working with children it is our responsibility to defend their rights.

There is a growing rhetoric from the Government that NGOs can play a more important role in resolving the problem of the poor. However, the spirit of this rhetoric is dubious. It is not that the Government believes that NGOs have magic solutions for solving the problems of the poor but it is rather shifting the State's responsibilities onto the NGOs due to the constraints put on them by the IMF and World Bank through their structural adjustment programmes. NGOs are being invited to take over and implement various social welfare programmes primarily because NGO strategies and approaches are effective and low cost. The Government is thus relieved of the burden of maintaining a huge infrastructure and permanent personnel by handing over the responsibility of looking after the needs of the poor to the NGOs. It therefore becomes even more imperative that we should form a strong alliance, an alliance that believes in the right of the child to a survival, protection, development, growth, participation and freedom of expression. A belief that whenever a child is denied his/her rights, it is a denial of human rights.

Ideas for Action

In order to turn the rhetoric and discussion into actions by NGOs, following could be considered any NGOs who are directly or indirectly concerned with the children and their well-being.

1. In all internal staff meetings discuss articles of the Convention related to the specific activities of your NGOs.

2. In all publications reproduce all/or relevant articles of the Convention.

3. Ensure all programme activities are so designed so as to relate to the relevant rights.

4. In all in-house training programmes include the theme/ module/session on Rights of the Child.

5. Use Rights of the Child as indicators for monitoring implementation and impact of your programme.

6. Arrange mechanisms for regular documentation on the violations of the rights of the children who are target beneficiaries of your programme.

7. In all programme contacts with adult--- parents, teachers, child care institution staff initiate discussion on the rights of the child.d

8. In all your activities, project and emphasize children as persons who have rights and are not merely passive

recipients of philanthropic and welfare activities.

9. Ensure that beneficiary children actively participate in planning, implementation and monitoring of activities directed to them.

10. As part of your programmes, include activities for social mobilization to promote greater sensitivity in communities and societies to Rights of the Child.

11. Participate actively in initiating and strengthening NGO networks on the subject of Child's Rights.

It is often said the health of a society is measured by the status of a child enjoys in his/her society.

I would like to end with a quotation from an open letter to the President of India which was written by 250 street and working children on behalf of 100 million child workers:

"Most often you adults do not realize that every act of yours has its effect on us. Whenever there is a riot, civil disturbance or war it is we children who suffer and bear the brunt of it. We are physically and emotionally traumatized every time a riot takes place. Our bodies do get healed but our emotion and minds take a long time to heal. Every night we go to sleep scared. We quite often hear that government is looking into these crimes but no one asks us as to what we feel nor do we know it the guilty are punished.

We do not want much from you but only our basic rights i.e. right to childhood. A child hood where we have opportunity and access to quality education, time to play, health care, food and protection from exploitation and oppression."

REFERENCES

UNICEF: "The Right to be a Child"; Unicef India Background Paper, March 1994, New Delhi.

Mengista Desta: "The Rights of the Child" published in Saksena K.P.(ed)" Human Rights: Perspective and Challenges; New

Delhi, Lanscers Book, 1994.

Phillips W.S.K. "Street Children in India"; Jaipur: Rawat Publications, 1994.

The World Human Development Report, 1994.

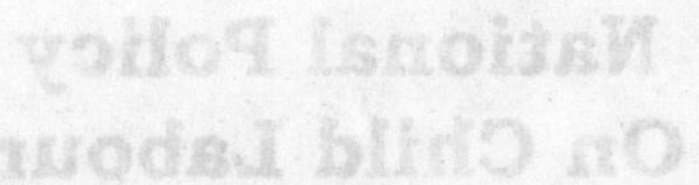

6

National Policy On Child Labour

1. Introduction

The Constitution of India, both in the Directive Principles of State Policy and as a part of the Fundamental Rights, has laid down that the State shall direct its policy towards securing that health and strength of workers, men and women, and the tender age of children are not abused, and that citizens are not forced by economic necessity to enter vocations unsuited to their age or strength, and that children, particularly, are given opportunities and facilities to develop in a healthy manner youth are to be protected against exploitation, and no in any factory or mine or engaged in any other hazardous employment.

The National Policy for Children Resolution, adopt in August, 1974, further developed the above ideas, and set out a policy framework and measures aimed at providing adequate services for children. These were to form a prominent part of the nation's plan for development all children upto the age of 14, provision alternative forms of education programmes and services, providing alternative advantage of formal school education for whatever reasons-and measures for protecting children against neglect, cruelty and exploitation form part of the National Policy for Children. The Policy also provides, as one of its objectives, that no child under the age of 14 years shall be permitted to be engaged in hazardous occupations or be made to undertake heavy work.

The Committee on Child Labour (Gurupadaswamy Committee) which submitted its report in December 1979, examined the problems of child labour in detail. India is one of the countries where the widespread existence of child labour has been viewed by the Government of India with concern. The Gurupadaswamy Committee recognized that a distinction had to be made between child labour and the exploitation of child labor as, through both are a that in all future action dealing with child labour this basic aspect would have to be taken note of, i.e., that "labour becomes an absolute evil in the case of the child when he is required to work beyond his physical capacity, when hours of employment interfere with his wages are not commensurate with the quantum of work done, and when the occupation he is engaged endangers his health and safety, i.e., when he is exploited.

Government has given consideration to these aspects of the problem of child labour, i.e., the need to protect child labour from exploitation or from being subjected to work in hazardous conditions which endanger such children's physical and mental development; the need to ensure safety and health at their working places; that they should be protected from excessively long working hours and from night work; and that there should be regulated work even in non-hazardous occupations, and that all child labour have to be provided with sufficient weekly rest periods and holiday in their employments.

The recently enacted Child Labour (Prohibition and

Regulation) Act, 1986, is the culmination of the process of consideration that Government has been giving to this pervasive problem figuring in the economic and social landscale in the country. Both in enacting this legislation, and thereafter in proceeding to lay down the policy and the outline of the programme of action, Government have had to keep in mind the economic and social aspects of child labour in the country. For example, with substantial portions of Gross Domestic Product (GDP) coming from the agricultural sector, from rural industries or from artisan's workshops, or from small scale services, often children work as an essential part of a farm household. or as a par t of the working family assisting parents in ancillary tasks. In such working activities by children in farm and field, in artisan households or in small family-centered trade or service establishments, children most often acquire the skills which enable them to become full-fledged workers in farming households, family establishments or trades. While work of such kinds has its problems, it is more essential at the present stage of our national development to concentrate in those sectors or establishments where children are deployed on wage or quasi-wage employment, outside the family, where there is most likely to arise exploitation, in whatever from it may be.

The national anti-poverty policies, the national education policy, the national policy on health for all and on nutrition, as also the generally stepped-up provisions in social services in national plan outlays, are all geared to tackle the problems of poverty, where too often the origins and compulsions of child labour are rooted. The general raising of large number of the population above the poverty line, or the provision of the entire spectrum of improved social services in the areas above mentioned will, it is hoped, lead to progressive elimination of poverty, and consequently of the phenomena of children being put out for wage employment or quasi-wage employment at unsuitable ages. The measures to promote employment oriented development and extension of adequate facilities for both formal and non-formal education, vocational education and training, and in the coverage and extension of social security and family welfare measures would all go a long way to tackle the basic and root causes of child labour.

This action programme, therefore, has to be viewed against the above background. Specifically, the attempt is to deal with a situation where children work, of are compelled to work, on a regular or a continuous basis to earn a living for themselves and/or for their family, and where their conditions of work result in their being severely dis-advantaged and exploited, and where abuses connected with such factors impacting on wage-employed children need to be given close attention by the State for rectification, amelioration and regulation through specific legal and administrative instruments and measures.

The future action programme is set out under the following three heads:

I. The Legislation Action Plan.

II. The focusing of general development programmes, for benefiting child labour wherever possible, and

III. Project-based Plan of Action in areas of high concentration of child labour engaged in wage/quasi-wage employment.

These are briefly set out below:

2. Legislation Action Plan

A Child Labour Technical Advisory Committee has been set up to advise the Central Government on addition of occupations and processes to the Schedule contained in Child Labour (Prohibition & Regulation) Act, 1986 (hereinafter referred to as CLA 86).

The provisions of the CLA 86, the Factories Act and the Mines Act will be enforced so as to particularly ensure that children are not employed in factories or mines or in any other hazardous employments or occupations, to ensure that the work is regulated in accordance with Part III of the CLA 86.

Where it is necessary for State Governments to make rules under CLA 86 or under any other legislation so as to protect the interests of child labour, they will be so requested to undertake reviews and frame rules as necessary. The Railway administration, major ports and Central and State Government departments incharge of oil-fields and mines will also similarly be asked to review the situation arising from the enactment of CLA 86, so as to ensure that child employments, and if employed in other occupations or employments, that the provisions set out for their health and safety, for the maintenance of registers, and for regulating the period and hours of work or overtime or of weekly holidays and days of rest are enforced in all establishments.

Government will also bring forward legislation to delete the provision contained in the Minimum Wages Act allowing different wages to be fixed for children, adolescents and adults. In other words, children will have to be paid the same as adults. This will remove the economic incentive to employ child labour on lower wages. For enforcing other protective legislation like the payment of Wages Act, the Equal of Gratuity Act, etc., it will be ensured that child labour is not discriminated against as compared to adult labour. The Central and State inspection machinery will be geared up for this purpose.

3. Focusing of General Development Programmes for Benefiting Child Labour

National development programmes exist with very wide coverage in areas of education, health, nutrition integrated child development and the anti-poverty group of programmes. In order to have an impact on child labor it will be necessary to focus these programmes by the implementing agencies under the State Government or the Central Government so as to deliver benefit to child labour wherever possible. Some areas where such focusing could be possible are set out below.

Education: The National Policy on Education, 1986

(NPF) sets the target of all children who attain the age of 11 years by 1990 having had five years of schooling, or its equivalent, through a non-formal system of education 4,90,000 non-formal education (NFE) centres are proposed to be opened which will supplement the formal educational system. Since the central feature of the implementation of the strategy for non-formal education is bases on micro-level and areas-specific and population-specific planning. NFE Centres for child labour will be set up with the involvement of voluntary agencies and Panchayati Raj institutions which are capable of running such non-formal education centres wherever possible to cater to child labour who, after work or during holidays can present themselves at the NEF centres. Special can present themselves at the NFE centres. Part-time courses and Vocational courses will also be catered to for at these centres. Such non-formal education centres for child labour would aim to educate children upto Class V level, with arrangements for continuance of non-formal education upto Class VIII wherever feasible. Where it is possible to organize such NFE centres for child labour, all the special features figuring in the Programme of Action of the NPE will be provided.

For child belonging to disadvantaged classes like SC/ST families, details of a scheme of to put out their children to wage / quasi-wage employment will be worked out in consultation with State Governments. For such children who come from families engaged in occupation like scavenging flaying and tanning, scholarships will be extended, with constant micro-planning and verification to ensure that SC/ST child labour in non-formal education centres are enrolled upto Class VIII. These are as per the specific provisions laid down in the Programme of Action of the NPE.

Micro planning for non-formal education centres will have to be undertaken for child labour, especially for those belonging to such disadvantaged sections of the society as SC/ST, or in areas where there are known to be concentration of such disadvantaged group of families.

In urban areas also, especially in urban slums, non-formal education programmes by both the State Governments and by voluntary agencies will be promoted, including the organization of extra-curricular activities, diversity in learning activity and with a provision of games and sports and related equipment, plays and skits, excursions, etc.

The projects of voluntary agencies will be entertained for a period of 3-4 years, whether for urban or for rural area, and while the initial proposals would be required to be sent to the State Governments, at subsequent stages, the voluntary agencies will directly approach the Department of Education centres. The Ministry of Labour may also arrange for micro-level planning for NFE centres for benefiting child labour, and recommended these to the Department of Education.

NREP/RLEGP funds would be used on a priority basis for creating the infrastructure for non-formal education centres catering to child labour under the overall coordination and direction of the local district level development authorities.

For continuing education of child labour who have been enrolled and successfully completed their period of non-formal education, efforts would be made to link the non-formal education institutions with the open schools, them to continue their education. The non-formal education programmes would also be linked with the Shramik Vidyapeeths, schemes of public libraries, Jana Shiksha Nilayams and Vocational and technical courses of a wide variety would be provided where required for among others, working children who come from the non-formal stream.

Health: Health is a State subject, and the programme of medical inspection of children has been assigned to the States. The progress among the various states is uneven. A few States have good programmes but many other States do not. In those States where there exists a school health service programme, many, and in some States even all, school-going children in the rural areas have been covered under the scheme for regular examinations. But those children who do not join school because of being at work would obviously not be covered by such school programme (where they exist). The Ministry of Health and Family Welfare will that address the State Governments, recommending that intensive medical inspection of children be taken up in those areas where child labour is prevalent. The State Governments will have to be persuaded to extend the coverage of the school health service programme to child labour. Since this is an area essentially under the State sector, a continuing dialogue, effort and persuasion with the State Governments will have to be maintained so that all children, irrespective of whether they are in primary school, or at work, are covered by regular health inspection and treatment/referral services. It should be possible to arrange for some health screening at NFE centres for child labour.

Nutrition: Department of Women and child Development have an on-going programme for women and children, i.e. Integrated Child Development Services which are approved on the basis of proposals by the State Governments and non-Governmental organizations. While it will not be possible to earmark funds specifically for child labour, proposals from State Governments/non Governmental organizations and voluntary agencies in child labour areas will be funded on a priority basis and, if necessary, the rules could be relaxed to consider proposals from the organizations to be set up for taking up welfare measures for child labour also.

Anti-Poverty Programmes Coverage: IRDP/NREP/RLEGP etc. fund are meant for poverty-alleviation programmes on the basis of criteria which have been laid down for the States to follow. Included in the coverage of the entire gamut of anti-poverty programmes are families which have child labour and, to the extent that such families with indigence of child labour fall within the selection criteria for endowment of income-generating assets (i.e. IRDP) or for wage employment (NREP/RLEGP) they would be benefited by the on-going programmes which have a large corpus of funds allocated to them in the 7th Plan. To the extent, therefore, that the poorest families are often faced to put out their children to work for wage/quasi-wage employment, they would be getting assistance to raise themselves above the poverty line and this, in conjunction with the non-formal education centres being opened in the rural areas, slum areas, etc. will go a long way towards tacking one of the basic causes of children being put to work i.e. poverty.

4. Project-Based Plan of Action

It is known that there are specific sectors of employment where the incidence of child labour is high, such as:

1. The match industry in Sivakasi, Tamil Nadu.
2. The diamond polishing industry in Surat, Gujarat.
3. The precious stone polishing industry in Jaipur, Rajasthan.
4. The glass industry in Ferozabad, Uttar Pradesh.
5. The brassware industry in Moradabad, Uttar Pradesh.
6. The handmade carpet industry in Mirzapur-Bhadohi in Uttar Pradesh.
7. The lock-making industry in Aligarh, Uttar Pradesh.
8. The handmade carpet industry in Jammu & Kashmir.
9. The slate pencil-making industry in Mandsaur, Madhya Pradesh.
10. The slate industry in Markapur in Andhra Pradesh.

The child workers involved in the above mentioned sectors of employment and geographical areas deserve priority attention because either the employments and processes in which they work are prohibited under the Factories Act, or the Child Labour (Prohibition and Regulation) Act, 1986 or the work is such that it is likely to affect the child's well-being.

In each of the 10 "project areas", the strategy will be to

evolve a package comprising of the following elements:

i) Stepping up the enforcement of the Child Labour (Prohibition and Regulation) Act, the Factories Act and the Mines Act. If necessary, special enforcement staff will be created for the purpose.

ii). Coverage of families of child labour under the income/employment generating programmes under the overall aegis of anti-poverty programmes.

iii). Where there is a concentration of SC/ST families with child labour, a concentration of special component and Tribal sub-plans by the State Governments in each project area.

iv). Formal/non-formal education of ultimately all child labour engaged in hazardous employment, and of as many child labour as possible as may be in non-hazardous employments. Also, a stepped up programme of adult education (including non-formal education) of the parents of the working children.

v). Coordinating the activities of different Departments/ Ministries of the Central Government and State Governments to benefit child labour.

vi). Setting up of special schools for child workers together with provision of vocational education/training in such special schools, supplementary nutrition, a stipend to the children taken out from prohibited employments, and health care for all children attending at such special schools.

For this purpose, i.e. the infrastructure will have to be created, and wherever the infrastructure run by the Departments of Education, Health, etc. like Shramik Vidya Peeth exists, they will be suitably modified and utilized. Stipends will not be paid to children who are working in non-hazardous/non-forbidden employments. The non-formal education/ formal educational institutions in the project area will function on flexible hour basis after working hours, during holidays, etc., as may be convenient. They will cover the range of special features of non-formal education set out in the Programme of Action of the NPE.

In order to enable intensive coverage in the Project areas of the anti-poverty group of programmes, the health programmes analogous to the school health programmes run by the State Governments, the special nutrition providing vocational education and training arrangements, and for providing stipends to the children taken out from hazardous employments, it will be necessary to provide for additionality of funds over and above the funds that exist in the respective programmes administered under the plan, whether by the Central Government or by State Governments. The additionality of funds required will be channeled through the Ministry of Labour, which will be nodal Ministry for the ten child projects.

In the first phase of the special project areas approach, it is proposed to cover upto 30,000 child labour. Each project will be carefully drawn up in consultation with the State Governments and Central Ministries concerned, to ensure proper coverage and inter-meshing of programmes administered by the Central and State Ministry of Labour. The Ministry of Labour will be the nodal agency for drawing up a project report in respect of each project area and for providing the additionality of funds that may be required for the total coverage envisaged in each project area.

5. Organization for Implementing the Child Labour Project

There will be a Chief Executive Officer in-charge of each project area who will work under the general supervision and the direction of the administrative head of the district wherein the project is situated. There will be a Child Labour Project Board, with the Collection as its Chairman on which it will be represented the district educational, health, and nutrition authorities, as also representatives of voluntary agencies/ Panchayati Raj institutions who are active in the district in the area of child labour. This will ensure coordination of all inputs of the various departments executing plan and non-plan schemes in the projects area, so as to enable the focusing allocate the additionality in project funds made available to each project by the Ministry of Labour.

6. Monitoring of Projects

The working of the child labour projects will be monitored by a high-powered Committee of the Central Government with representatives of the Ministry/Departments, of Labour , Education, Health, Rural Development, Child and Women Development and th State Governments where child labour projects are being implemented, namely, Tamil Nadu, Uttar Pradesh, Rajasthan, Gujarat, Jammu & Kashmir, Madhya Pradesh and Andhra Pradesh. The Committee will meet as often as necessary to ensure the smooth working of the project.

THE CHILD LABOUR (PROHIBITION OF REGULATION) ACT, 1986

[Act No. 61 of 1986]

[23rd December, 1986]

An Act to prohibit the engagement of children in certain employments and to regulate the conditions of work of children in certain other employments.

Be it enacted by Parliament in the Thirty-seventh Year of the Republic of India as follows:

PRELIMINARY

1. Short title, extent and commencement.-

1) This Act may be called the Child Labour (Prohibition and Regulation) Act, 1986.

2) It extends to the whole India.

3) The provisions of this Act, other than Part III, shall come

into force at once, and Part III shall come into force on such date as the Central Government may, by notification in the Official Gazette, appoint and different dates may be appointed for different States and for different classes of establishments.

2. Definitions- In this Act, unless the context otherwise requires-

(i) "appropriate Government" means, in relation to as establishment under the control of the Central Government or a railway administration or a major port or a mine or oil field, the Central Government, and in all other cases, the State Government;

(ii) "child" means a person who has not completed his fourteenth year or age;

(iii) "day" means a period of twenty-four hours beginning at mid-night;

(iv) "establishment" includes a shop, commercial establishment, workshop, farm, residential hotel, restaurant, eating house, theater or other place of public amusement or entertainment;

(v) "family", in relation to an occupier, means the individual, the wife or husband, as the case may be, of such individual, and their children, brother or sister of such individual;

(vi) "Occupier", in relation to an establishment or a workshop, means the person who has the ultimate control over the affairs of the establishment or workshop.

(vii) "port authority" means any authority administering a port;

(viii) "prescribed" means prescribed by rules made under section 18;

(ix) "week" means a period of seven days beginning at midnight on Saturday night or such other night as may be approved in writing for a particular area by the inspector;

(x) "workshop" means any premises (including the precincts thereof) wherein any industrial process is carried on, but not include any premises to which the provisions of section 67 of the Factories Act, 1948, for the time being apply.

PROHIBITION OF EMPLOYMENT OF CHILDREN IN CERTAIN OCCUPATIONS AND PROCESSES

Prohibition of employment of children in certain occupation processes.- No. child shall be employed or permitted to work in any of the occupations set forth in Part A of the Schedule or in any workshop wherein any of the processes set forth in Part B of the Provided that nothing in this section shall apply to any workshop wherein any process is carried on by the occupier with the aid of his family or to any school established by, or receiving assistance or recognition from Government.

Power to amend the Schedule.- The Central Government, after giving by notification in the Official Gazette, not less than three months notice of its intention so to do, may, by like notification, add any occupation or process to the Schedule and thereupon the Schedule shall be deemed to have been amended accordingly.

Child Labour Technical Advisory Committee- (1) The Central Government may, by notification in the Official Gazette, constitute an advisory committee to be called the Child Labour Technical Advisory Committee (hereafter in this section referred to as the Committee) to advise the Central Government for the purpose of addition of occupation and processes to the Schedule.

(2) The Committee shall consist of a Chairman and such other members not exceeding ten, as may be appointed by the Central Government.

(3) The Committee shall meet as often as it may consider necessary and shall have power to regulate its own procedure.

(4) The Committee may, if it deems it necessary so to do, constitute one or more sub-committee and may appoint to any such sub-committee, whether generally or for the consideration of

any particular matter, any person who is not a member of the Committee.

(5) The term of office of, the manner of filling casual vacancies in the office of and the allowances, if any, payable to the Chairman and other members of the Committee, and the conditions and restrictions subject to which the Committee may appoint any person who is not a member of the Committee as a member of any of its sub-committees shall be such as may prescribed.

REGULATION OF CONDITIONS OF WORKS OF CHILDREN

Application of Part- The provisions of this Part shall apply to an establishment or a class of establishment in which none of the occupation or processes referred to in section 3 is carried on.

Hours and period of work.- (1) No child shall be required or permitted to work in any establishment in excess of such number of hours as may be prescribed for such establishment or class of establishments.

(2) The period of work on each day shall be so fixed that no period shall exceed three hours before he has had an interval for rest for at least one hour.

(3) The period of work of child shall be so arranged that inclusive of his interval for rest, under sub-section (2), it shall not be spread over more than six hours, including the time spent in writing for work on any day.

(4) No child shall be permitted or required to work between 7 p.m. and 8 a.m.

(5) No child shall be required or permitted to work overtime.

(6) No child shall be required or permitted to work in any establishment on any day on which he has already been working in another establishment.

Weekly holidays.- Every child employed in an establishment shall be allowed in each week, a holiday of one whole day, which day shall be specified by the occupier in a notice permanently exhibited in a specified shall not be altered by the occupier more than once in three months.

Notice to Inspector.- (1) Every occupier in relation to an establishment in which a child was employed or permitted to work immediately before the data of commencement of this Act in relation to such establishment shall, within a period of thirty days from such commencement, send to the Inspector within whose local limits the establishment is situated, a written notice containing the following particulars, namely:

(a) the name and situation of the establishment;

(b) the name of the person in actual management of the establishment;

(c) the address to which communications relating to the establishment should be sent; and

(d) the nature of the occupation or process carried on in the establishment.

(2) Every occupier, in relation to an establishment, who employee, or permits to work, any child after the data of commencement of this Act in relation to such establishment, shall, within a period of thirty days from the date of such employment, send to the Inspector within whose local limits the establishment is situated, a written notice containing the particulars as are mentioned in sub-section (1).

Explanation - For the purpose of sub-sections (1) and (2), "date of commencement of this Act, in relation to an establishment" means the date of bringing into force of this Act in relation to such establishment.

(3) Nothing in sections 7, 8 and 9 shall apply to any establishment wherein any processes is carried on by the occupier with the aid of his family or to any school establishment by, or

receiving assistance or recognition from, Government.

Disputes as to age.- If any question arises between an Inspector and an occupier as to the age of any child who is employed or is permitted to work by him in an establishment, the question shall, in the absence of a certificate as to the age of such child granted by the prescribed medical authority, be referred by the Inspector for decision to the prescribed medical authority.

Maintenance of register.- There shall be maintained by every occupier in respect of children register or permitted to work in any establishment, a register to be available for inspection by an Inspector at all times during working hours or when work is being carried on in any such establishment, showing-

(a) the name and date of birth of every child so employed or permitted to work;

(b) hours and periods of work of any such child and the intervals of rest to which he is entitled;

(c) the nature of work of any such child; and

(d) such other particulars as may be prescribed.

Display of notice containing abstract of sections 3 and 14.- Every railway administration, every port authority and every occupier shall cause to be displayed in a conspicuous and accessible place at every station on its railway or within the limits of a port or at the place of work, as the case may be, a notice in the local language and in the English language containing an abstract of sections 3 and 14.

Health and safety.- (1) The appropriate Government may, by notification in the Official Gazette, make rules for the health and safety of the children employed or permitted to work in any establishment or class of establishments.

(2) Without prejudice to the generality of the foregoing provisions, the said rules may provide for all or any of the following matters, namely:-

(a) cleanliness in the place of work and its freedom from nuisance;
(b) disposal of wastes and effluents;
(c) ventilation and temperature;
(d) dust and fume;
(e) artificial humidification;
(f) lighting;
(g) drinking and urinals;
(h) latrine and urinals;
(i) spittoons;
(j) fencing of machinery;
(k) work at or near machinery in motion;
(l) employer of children on dangerous machines;
(m) instruction, training and supervision in relation to employment of children on dangerous machines;
(n) device for cutting off power;
(o) self-acting machines;
(p) easing of new machinery;
(q) floor, stairs and means of access;
(r) pits, sumps, openings in floors, etc.;
(s) excessive weights;
(t) protection of eyes;
(u) explosive or inflammable dust, gas, etc.;
(v) precautions in case of fire;
(w) maintenance of buildings; and
(x) safety of buildings and machinery.

MISCELLANEOUS

Penalties - (1) Wherever employs any child or permits any child to work in contravention of the provisions of section 3 shall be punishable with imprisonment for a term which shall not be less than three month but which may extend to one year or with fine which shall not be less than ten thousand rupees but which may extend to twenty thousand rupees or with both.

(2) Whoever, having been convicted of an offense under sec-

tion 3, commits a like offense afterwards, the shall be punishable with imprisonment for a term which shall not be less than six months but which may extend to two years.

(3) Whoever-

(a) fails to give notice as required by section or

(b) fails to maintain a register as required by Section 11 or makes any false entry in any such register; or

(c) fails to display a notice containing an abstract of section 3 and this section as required by section 12; or

(d) fails to comply with or contravenes any other provisions of this Act or the rules made thereunder.Shall be punishable with imprisonment which may extend to one month or with fine which may extend to ten thousand rupees or with both.

Modified application of certain laws in relation to penalties.- (1) Where any person is found guilty and convicted of contravention of any of the provisions mentioned in sub-section (2), he shall be liable to penalties as provided in sub-sections (1) and (2) of section 14 of this Act and not under the Acts in which those provisions are contained.

(2) The provisions referred to in sub-section (1) are the provisions mentioned below:

(a) section 67 of the Factories Act, 1948;

(b) section 40 of the Mines Act, 1952;

(c) section 109 of the Merchant Shipping Act, 1958; and

(d) section 21 of the Motor Transport Workers Act, 1961.

Procedure relating to offenses.- (1) Any person, police officer or Inspector may file a complaint of the commission of any offense under this Act in any court of competent jurisdiction.

(2) Every certification as to the age of a child which has been granted by a prescribed medical authority shall, for the purpose of this Act, be conclusive evidence as to the age of the

child to whom it relates.

(3) No court inferior to that of a Metropolitan Magistrate or a Magistrate of the first class shall try any offense under this Act.

Appointment of inspectors.- The appropriate Government may appoint Inspectors for the purpose of securing compliance with the provisions of this Act and any Inspector so appointed shall be deemed to be a public servant within meaning of the Indian Code.

Power to make rules.- (1) The appropriate Government may, by notification in the Official Gazette and subject tot he condition of previous publication, make rule for carrying into effect the provisions of this Act.

(2) In particular and without prejudice to the generality of the foregoing power, such rules may provide for all or any of the following matters, namely:-

(a) the term of office of the manner of filling casual vacancies of, and the allowance payable to, the Chairman and members of the Child Labour Technical Advisory Committee and the conditions and restrictions subject to which a non-member may be appointed to a sub-committee under sub-section (5) of section 5;

(b) number of hours for which a child may be required or permitted to work under sub-section (1) of section 7;

(c) grant of certificates of age in respect of young persons in employment or seeking employment, the medical authorities which may issue such certificate, the form of such certificate, the charges which may be made thereunder and the manner in which such certificate may be issued:

provided that no charge shall be made for the issue of any such certificate if the application is accompanied by evidence of age deemed satisfactory by the authority concerned;

(d) the other particulars which a register maintained under

section 11 should contain.

Rules and notifications to be laid beforc Parliament or State legislation.- (1) Every rule made under this Act by the Central Government and every notification issued under section4, shall be laid as soon as may be after it is made or issued for a total period of thirty days which may be comprised in one session or in two or more successive sessions, and before the expiry of the session immediately the session or the successive sessions aforesaid, both Houses or the making any modification in the rule or notification should not be made or issued, the rule or notification shall thereafter have effect only in such modified form or be of no effect, as the case may be; so, however, that any such validity of anything previously one under that rule or notification.

(2) Every rule made by a State Government under this Act shall be laid as soon as may be after it is made, before the legislation of that State.

Certain other provisions of law not barred.- Subject to the provisions contained in section 15, the provisions of this Act and rules made thereunder shall be in addition to, and not in derogation of, the provisions of the Factories Act, 1948 the Plantations Labour Act, 1951 and the Mines Act, 1952

Power to remove difficulties.- (1) If any difficulty arises in giving effect to the provisions of this Act, the Central Government may, by order published in the Official Gazette, make such provisions not inconsistent with the provisions of this Act as appear to it to be necessary or expedient for removal of the difficulty.

Provided that no such order shall be made after the expiry of a period of three years from the date on which this Act receives the assent of the President.

(2) Every order made under this section shall, as soon as may be after it is made, be laid before the Houses of Parliament.

Repeal and savings.- (1) The Employment of Children Act,

1938 is hereby repealed.

(2) Notwithstanding such repeal, anything done or any action taken or purported to have been done or taken under the Act so repealed shall, in so far as it is not inconsistent with the provisions of this Act, be deemed to have been done or taken under the corresponding provisions of this Act.

Amendment of Act 11 of 1948.- In Section 2 of the Minimum Wages Act, 1948-

(i) for clause (a), the following clauses shall be substituted, namely:-

(a) "adolescent" means a person who has completed his fourteenth year of age but has not completed his eighteenth year;

(aa) "adult" means a person who has completed his eighteenth year of age;";

(ii) after clause (b), the following clause shall be inserted, namely:-

(bb) "child" means a person who has not completed his fourteenth year of age'.

Amendment of Act 69 of 1951.- In the Plantation Labour Act, 1951-

(a) in Section 2, in clauses (a) and (c), for the word "fifteenth," the word "fourteenth" shall be substituted;

(b) Section 24 shall be omitted;

(c) in Section 26, in the opening portion, the words "who has completed his twelfth year" shall be omitted.

Amendment of Act 44 of 1958.- In the Merchant Shipping Act, 1958, in Section 109, for the word "fifteenth", the word "fourteenth" shall be substituted.

Amendment of Act 27 of 1961.- In the Motor Transport Workers Act, 1961, in Section 2, clauses (a) and (c), for the word "fifteenth", the word "fourteenth" shall be substituted.

THE SCHEDULE (See Section 3)

PART A

Occupations

Any occupation connected with-

(1) Transport of passengers, goods or mails by railway;

(2) Cinder picking, clearing of an ash pit or building operation in the railway premises;

(3) Work in a catering establishment at a railway station, involving the movement of a vendor or any other employee of the establishment from one platform to another or into or out of a moving train;

(4) Work relating to the construction of a railway station or with any other work where such work is done in close proximity to or between the railway lines;

(5) A port authority within the limits of any port.

PART B

Processes

(1) Bidi-making.
(2) Carpet-weaving.
(3) Cement, manufacture, including bagging of cement.
(4) Cloth printing, dyeing and weaving.
(5) Manufacture of matches, explosives and fire-works.
(6) Mica-cutting and splitting.
(7) Shellac manufacture.
(8) Soap manufacture.
(9) Tanning.
(10) Wool-cleaning.
(11) Building and construction industry.

7

Consequences of Child Labour : Education and Health

Introduction

When children work, both their education and health suffer. How does this happen? The Indian school system has a single point entry and consists of a sequential and full-time format of institutional instruction by full-time and professional teachers. One of the most comprehensive critiques of such a system in relation to the circumstances and needs of rural and agricultural society has been formulated by the noted educationist, the late J.P.Naik. He argues for a radical transformation in the traditional model of formal education. Despite the advantages of the single point entry method such as the creation of the homogeneous age-group cohort which rises, year after year, to successively higher classes, it means that the child who is unable to enter school at class I at the age of six years remains outside it forever. Though in principle the same child could enter class I at age eleven years, he would have to be with much younger children and despite his readiness to go faster, he would have to learn at the same speed. Most likely he would become a drop out. Naik (1975a) says:

What such a child need is specially organized classes where primary education is imparted through special techniques suited to his more mature mind. But there is no provision in our system for this purpose.

J.P.Naik recommends a multiple-entry point at different ages say nine, eleven, fourteen and so on. According to him, an elastic schooling system which permits children to enter it as and when they wish to or are in a position to do so would attract large numbers of children who would otherwise have remained illiterate. Naik makes a number of constructive suggestions to orient the school system to the needs of rural working children. For one thing, the school calendar should be so adjusted as to allow time off for agricultural operations like sowing and harvesting; for another, to reduce stagnation on account of children failing examinations, flexible systems which condense the curricula of classes i to iv into a shorter period of about two years for children over eleven could be devised. Another important recommendation he makes is to have pre-schools or creches attached to primary schools so that girls could bring their younger siblings there and look after them, as well as get an education. Instead of relying upon full-time professional teachers who raise the costs of the school system, Naik suggests simple solutions like employing local carpenters, tailors, singers and young persons who could teach for part of the time. Such a step would also generate additional local employment at lower cost. In summary, Naik's contribution has been to suggest that the school system be re-oriented to cater to the needs of working children in an agricultural society in a practicable way and at a low cost.

The lack of adequate infrastructure apart, the mos common explanation for parents not sending their children t

school is that they are too poor. It is argued that the economic contribution of the child to the income of the family-whether by bringing in a wage or by doing household maintenance work and thus releasing adults for productive work-is so important that the family cannot afford to lose this economically productive work-is so important that the family cannot afford to lose this economically productive time for his or her schooling. Clearly, there is some substance in such reasoning, as poor families exist on the mar-
gins, of survival.

Yet, such an argument fails to take into account the exploitation by vested interests of young children. Many studies document the role of vested interests and the impact they have upon the lives of children. It is also true that working children in India, by and large, belong to the poor regions of the country, the socially disadvantaged sections of society and some minority groups. There is a vested interest in seeing that the children of the poor do not avail themselves of the facilities for education. Large numbers of children are lured away from schools by middlemen who offer a better life if they agree to work. In what follows, examples are given from the match and carpet industries of how this process operates. This probably happens in other industries using child labour, but very little documented evidence was available. My own research in the five industries of glass, brass, lock, gems pottery did not look at this aspect in great depth.

VESTED INTERESTS

In many of the large concentrations of child labour in India-such as Sivakasi in the State of Tamil Nadu-where the match industry is housed and where approximately 45,000 children are working, Smitu Kothari, a social activist, observes that '...In village after village we found cases where children were induced to leave school to support the family economically' (Kothari 1983b).

The educational status of children in the match factories

of Sivakasi is dismal. UNICEF supported a sample study to investigate it. They conducted their survey in sixteen factories which were employing 4725 children. Of these 4725 workers, 544 were working at home. The figures are startling as they reveal that of the 4181 children studied, 3323 or 79 per cent were totally illiterate. Children numbering 474 or 11 per cent of the sample had received education up to the primary level. There were 384 drop outs accounting for the balance 9 per cent. When the research team looked at the wage register, they found that 81 per cent of the children had received payments after affixing their thumb impressions and only 19 per cent had signed their names. Thus in one of the largest concentrations of child labour, Sivakasi, nearly 80 per cent of the children were illiterate and most of them came to the factories form the rural areas in factory buses which left the village at 3 a.m. or 4 a.m. to return only after dusk. These children, mainly girls, are from Scheduled Castes and work ten to fourteen hours a day at break-neck speed in order to earn a pittance of Rs 2 or 3 per cent day (Area Development Report). The average age of the working child is between eight to twelve years. According to the Area Development Report, 'It looks as though the mid-day-meals programme is the chief motivational link for most children to attend school in an irregular fashion'.

If one looks at the educational status of children working in the carpet factories, the situations is similar. Prembhai, a social worker, was asked by the Supreme Court of India to investigate the incidence of bonded child labour in the carpet industry of Mirzapur-Bhadohi-Varanasi in the State of Uttar Pradesh. He interviewed 858 children who had migrated from the adjoining district of Palamau in the State of Bihar and found that only one child had been to high school. Thirteen children (one and 1/2 per cent) had been educated from class iv to viii. Sixty-five children (8 per cent) had received education from class II to class V; seventeen children (2 per cent) were barely literate. And the bulk of 762 children, that is almost 89 per cent, were completely illiterate (Prembhai 1984).

School authorities in the carpet belt are extremely concerned that children are being sent to work rather than to school. Parent are being bribed by middlemen with small consumption loans and an assurance that the child will learn a skill; they are then made to work fourteen to sixteen hours a day under the most unhygienic conditions which are also akin to semi-slavery. The situation in the carpet belt of Mirzapur-Bhadohi-Varanasi is so grim that local teachers were really concerned about what would happen to those children who were being made to leave school in large numbers. Prembhai observes in his report that teachers, educational administrators and village elders all reacted negatively to the impact of the industry. People told him that **harijans** were taking their children out of school to enter the industry and there was a discernible trend in the migration of children to those areas where the industry operated. One **harijan** leader told him that the industry was blocking the development of **harijans** and promoting illiteracy amongst them.

There are approximately 150,000 children working as carpet weavers in the Mirzapur-Bhadohi carpet belt (Juyal 1987). The number of working children in the carpet belt went up when the Government of India set up carpet training centres in the Mirzapur area and other places and offered a stipend of Rs 60 month to the trainees. A large number of children were forced by their parents to leave school and join the training institutes (Menon 1986). Once the children had dropped out of school, there was no question of returning. When there was a slump in the carpet industry, these children were the first to be retrenched. These illiterate or semi-literate children were forced to take on jobs in roadside restaurants, as domestic servants and so on.

The match industry of Sivakashi and the carpet industry of Mirzapur-Bhadohi-Varanasi are both illustrations of the consequences of using children for their labour. It is not accidental that in both cases the children concerned belong to the socially lowest segment of society, i.e. the Scheduled Castes;

these children are forced into relations of bondage with their employers, who suborn the parents by advancing small sums of money by way of loans and the children are bounded till the loan is returned at usurious rates of interest. Apart from the exploitative working environment, one glaring result of children's work is their almost complete illiteracy.

CLASS BIAS IN EDUCATION

It is demonstrable that children who work belong to the lowest strata of society and children who stay out school also belong to the lowest rung in the class structure. Poromesh Acharya, in a study of child labour in four villages of two districts of West Bengal, found that of the total non-enrolled children in the age-group six to sixteen years, 70 per cent belonged to the two lowest agrarian classes, namely poor peasants and agricultural labourers (Acharya 1982). Though the situation may well have changed for the better today, the statistics are revealing.

According to Acharya, more than 92 per cent of one set of respondents (who were lower middle and poor peasants as also agricultural labourers) replied to the relevant question by saying that their non-enrolled children were either gainfully employed or did household work during school hours.

Acharya makes an important statement regarding the attitude of the upper strata of rural society towards free compulsory education. He explains the oppositions towards making elementary education compulsory by referring to the fear of the jotedars and the rich peasants that the traditional order would be disturbed. He observes that the continuing illiteracy of the labouring groups helps the reinforcement of the traditional patterns of authority in village life.

Acharya's study found that the rich peasants did not want compulsory education because it would be inconvenient for them although all the children of the **jotedars** in the age group six to eleven years and 84 per cent of the children of the rich peasants of the same age-group were enrolled. Acharya does not mince words when he says:

The reasons are very simple. They are against compulsion as they fear that universal and compulsory enrollment would deprive them of the easy supply of child labour. In that case, they would need to hire adults at a higher wage instead of child labour, which would lead to an increase in their cost of agricultural production.

U.P.Arora also has similar observation to make regarding the need for child labour by rich peasants in the State of Karnataka. Arora argues that teenagers are subjected to **jeeta** (bonded labour) by landlords because they are always available for any type of work. He notes that the wards and relations of landlords increasingly go to the towns and cities to pursue a higher education and,consequently, there is a demand for more working hands (Arora et.al. 1977).

Other studies are also pointers to local vested interests who do not want the children of the poor to get an education. The Rural Wing of the National Labour Institute conducted a study on bonded labour. Investigators interviewed some owners of bonded labourers in Andhra Pradesh about education for working children. Their response was:

Once,they are allowed to come up to an equal level, nobody will go to the fields. Fields will be left uncultivated everywhere. We have to keep them under our strong thumb in order to get work done (NLI Rural Wing 1977).

As in the case of unorganized industry, the cases cited above from backward sectors of the agricultural economy bring out the importance of the need of upper segments of the population to maintain illiteracy and thereby their hold on a docile and submissive labour force. When one studies the links between child labour and education, it is helpful to remember the social contexts in which child labour flourishes at the expense of the education. The working child suffers from the spiraling disadvantages of being illiterate, coming from economically poor classes and belonging to socially backward communities.

WORKING CHILDREN AND SCHOOLS

There is a point of view frequently propounded by professionals in the field of education and policy-makers that the existing school system is irrelevant to the needs of working children. It is argued that sterile curricula, rote-based learning and the poor quality of teachers, amongst others ills, plague the school system and that, therefore, neither the parents of working children nor the children themselves are keen to gain access to it. I have tried to argue that this is a profoundly mistaken idea. Rather, evidence from the field suggests that parents have a deep interest in educating their children. Education alone can provide mobility to the socially and economically disadvantaged sections of society. More correctly it is straightened economic circumstances which prevent the fulfillment of this aspiration; inadequate school infrastructure tilts the balance in favour of work.

In all the industries I had the opportunity of studying, it was clear that the children of the master craftsmen and the better-off artisans went to school regularly and spent perhaps a couple of hours a day learning the trade. It was the children of the lowest level of workers, the underemployed or of the unemployed who did not attend school and constituted the bulk of the child labour force. By and large such children belonged either to the Scheduled Castes, lower castes or the Muslim community. These groups represented a combination of economic and social disadvantages. When one looked at the lives of these children as they grew to adulthood, it was apparent that the absence of schooling closed the route to upward mobility and, once again, perpetuated the desadvantage in the next generation. Interview after interview, without exception, revealed widespread awareness about the importance of an education to improve the prospects of children. Almost to a man my respondents have great aspirations for their children but the absence of an adequate school infrastructure offering quality education combined with the costs of schooling served to deny them the fulfillment of their hopes. In the cases where the economic circumstances of the worker improved because of some reason or the other, the first thing they did was to remove their children from the work-force and put them into school even if they substituted them with children of an even poorer group. It would seem then to be a myth, sometimes sedulously cultivated, that poor parents are simply not interested in a formal education for their children. In every industry workers knew about how section of the better-off,like the entrepreneur, the trader and the exporter, send their children to school to learn English so that they would be able to deal better with the outside world.

IMPACT ON HEALTH

It is ironical that the conservative approaches of experts have grown with fresh information regarding the deleterious effects of work on the health of Young children. Many discussions on health hazards for working children start with opening statements like: 'Not all work is hazardous to children' (Gore 1985) or 'work' can in fact be beneficial to the child' (Pitt 1985a). More recently, an important study conducted in Bombay has argued that working children are in fact healthier than non-working children because of the food they get to eat. In fairness, it must also be said that those who have written extensively about health hazards to working children and have argued that not all work is harmful (Pitt 1985b) have also admitted that not enough information is available on the subject.

By and large children who are examined at the work-site are amongst the fittest. What about those who have fallen by the wayside-injured or ill or even dead as a result of overwork, exhaustion and so on? I shall try to establish the significance of such omission later in the chapter. To leave them out of the count is to be unscientific and leads to a distorted version of the facts. Such selectivity leads to what may be termed the 'pragmatic' view increasingly favoured these days by experts. This pragmatism bodes ill for the vision of health as a fundamental human right.

This chapter seeks to draw attention to the different types of hazards faced by working children and proposes a scheme of classification for them. Firstly, children are employed in intrinsically hazardous occupations where they may contract silicosis, pneumoconiosis, byssinosis, etc. by working in the slate, lock, glass and power loom industries, for example.

Secondly, some hazards find their origin in the poor working environment. Thirdly, a few occupations may be considered safe but the vulnerability of children makes these occupations hazardous for them. Hence, one has to examine (a) whether hazards are intrinsic to the nature of the work itself or (b) whether they arise from the working environment and conditions of work or (c) whether the work is simply unsuitable for children.

Any occupation which allows the worker to come into contact with harmful substances like chemicals (as in the balloon, match and fire-works, lock and brass ware industries) or fire (as in the glass industry) or cotton fluff and dust that damage the lungs (as in the power loom industry) may be termed intrinsically hazardous. These occupations would be hazardous for all workers, both adults and children. But since children are still in the process of growing and attaining their full physical stature, their growth is likely to be affected. We will now consider some examples of intrinsically hazardous occupations.

The Balloon Factories of Dahanu

In the balloon factories of Dahanu in Maharashtra, children's work includes mixing rubber with chemicals,coloring balloons and testing each balloon with gas. A thick pall of dust and chemicals pervades the rooms which are small, cramped and ill-ventilated. According to Geeta Menon, the children work nine hours a day, six days a week,'Medical reports state that inhalation of such acids continuously over a period of time can burn respiratory lining and cause pneumonia, bronchopneumonia, cough, breathlessness and even heart failure....(Menon 1985).

A more recent newspaper article reported that when visitors visited the balloon factories of Dahanu, they were told not to enter for fear of choking on the ammonia fumes (Sharma 1992). The children who work there have to inhale ammonia, ascetic acid fumes and french chalk for more than eight hours a day and six days a week. Some children are barely eight years old!

The Match Industry of Sivakasi

Vishwapriya Iyengar writes about the health hazards to children in the match industry of Sivakasi in Tamil Nadu.

Children mixing chemicals in the boiler room get lung fulls of toxic fumes, suffer high degrees of intense heat and run the risk of being badly injured in fire accidents. Children who stamps frames on the metal sheet too suffer heat, toxic fumes and excessive strain on the arms and shoulders which have to remove and place the heavy frames with great rapidity. Delay of a second... can cause the entire frame to go up in roaring flames which cause instant death (Iyengar 1986a).

Smitu Kothari, writing about the match and fireworks industry, says that the working conditions are unsafe and detrimental to the health and well-being of children. Children are away fifteen hours a day, of which twelve are spent working in cramped environmental with hazardous chemicals and inadequate ventilation. Says Kothari:

Dust from the chemicals powders and strong vapours in both

the store room and the boiler room were obvious at practically every site we visited' (Kothari 1983c).

The match industry of Sivakasi is one the most hazardous industries in the country where children work. Children interviewed by researchers tell about the strain of heat and the heavy frames which make them feel dizzy and faint. The children have to be very alert or else there is a danger that they will set fire to themselves. Fire accidents occur when the match heads rub against the frictional surface in the course of putting the box together too quickly (Iyengar 1987).

The main risk in the match industry is a result of the chemicals used. The Area Development Programme Report for Ramanathapuram district, which was prepared for UNICEF, lists a wide variety of chemicals used in the match industry. These include tetrophosphorous trisulphide, amorphous red phosphorous, potassium chlorate, antimony trisulphikde, zince oxide, calcium sulphate and so on (Area Development Report).

Given the kinds of chemicals used,it is not surprising that accidents are frequent (**The Hindu,** 31 January 1988).

The fire-works factories are particularly dangerous. It is only when newspapers report accidents that we hear of the health hazards in the industry. Kothari reports that in February,1982,a cracker factory in Chellapathi village, twenty kilometers from Sankaran Koil, went up in flames. Six children were charred to death in the fire. They had been engaged in stuffing cracker powder into fire-crackers when the accident occurred (Kothari 1983c). In another accident thirty-two children were burnt to death in an electrical fire in a cracker factory (Singh 1982). More recently in July 1991, thirty-six people were killed in a blast in a fire-works factory near Meenampatti village about five kilometers from Sivakasi. Within seconds about fifteen buildings of the factory were charred. The newspaper reported that the minimum age of the victims was sixteen years. But even if they were younger, the bodies were beyond recognition and neither parents or employers would admit of child labour in a banned industry. The proprietor, of course, fled the scene of action (*The Hindu*,12 July 1991).

Not only are working conditions hazardous, the children are brought from home in factory buses at 3 a.m. in the morning. The buses are packed to the brim. In an accident, thirty-seven children lost their lives when a bus, over-loaded with child workers, was swept off in the river Arjuna in a flash flood at Thirumagal. Interestingly, when the bus was stuck under a bridge the children wanted to get out but were prevented from doing so in order to prevent the bus from being swept away in the flood (Garg 1980). Gurbir Singh (1982) reports that after the bus tragedy, Mrs. Jayalaxmi, a Lok Sabha (Lower House of the Indian Parliament) member, had called for a probe into the Sivakasi industries alleging that the number of deaths was very high. She said, 'the agents of the factory buy the parents off and conduct mass cremation or mass burial in some secluded places.'

The attempt of employers is to pay a paltry sum to the parents and hush up the incident. Accidents in the match and fire-works industry are fairly frequent though they do not get reported because of the political vested interests of the employers who are able to contain the information locally. But researchers in the field tell another story.

A review of the literature from other industries shows that similar types of health hazards exist in other industries as well. In many industries-such as power looms-workers suffer from byssinosis. This disease is caused by cotton dust and fibre which get embedded in the lining of the lungs and cause fibrosis of the tissue. This reduces the normal capacity of the lungs and puts pressure on the surviving tissues. A patient of byssinosis is highly susceptible to bronchitis and tuberculosis. There are an estimated 15,000 children working in the powerloom industy of Bhiwandi in Maharashtra (Barse 1985).

The State Pencil Industry of Mandsaur

In Mandsaur district, Madhya Pradesh, where the slate industry is housed, silicosis is a very common occupational disease among the workers. The verdict of a team of doctors headed by the Mandsaur hospital's civil surgeon, Dr J.N.Narodia, is that there is no cure for silicosis. Dr. Narodia explains how and why silicosis is dangerous:

Silicon dust is very light and flies about, unlike, say, coal dust in a coal mine which is heavier and falls to the ground. The silicon dust rises and enters the lungs, forming silica patches. This reduces the elasticity of the lungs, causing fibrosis. As a result the vital capacity of the lungs, that is the oxygen exchange rate, is reduced, since the surface area which absorbs oxygen is less due to the silica patches. The patient does not get oxygen and develops symptoms of chest diseases, like TB. If the patches are large enough the person suffocates to death. The only treatment possible is not for silicosis but to check secondary infections like pneumonia, etc. (Mitra 1986).

Approximately 1000 children are employed in Mandsaur (Rao 1980: 1983) and cut plates of shale into small pieces with electrically operated saws, a process which emits dense clouds of a fine, light dust that the workers constantly inhale. The result is silicosis or pneumoconiosis, a lung disease similar to, but much deadlier than tuberculosis. According to Amiya Rao:

The medical check-up conducted by the Social Service Club of Indore earlier in 1980 has revealed that most of the child workers have got this disease (silicosis) and will soon die. 'We can't do a thing', says the Civil Surgeon. 'The disease causes fibrous changes in the lungs. Lungs are gradually eaten away, patients suffer respiratory trouble, being to spit blood and then die a painful death'.

Nirmal Mitra reports:

Children at the age of twelve and even less, are forced into the fatal work to sustain their dying parents, brothers and sisters, only to learn that they will die soon enough too-of the dust, fatigue and inhumanity. The story has been repeated year after year, for five decades now (Mitra 1986).

The enormity of the health hazards can be appreciated when it is realized that in the village of Multanpura, which has

60 per cent of all the slate pencil factories in Mandsaur, there is hardly any old person and almost every third women is widowed. They are known as 'pollution widows' because their husbands have died from inhaling the slate dust. Most of the workers in this industry will choke to death before reaching forty years of age.

Other Industries

Ninety-five per cent of the respondents in a study conducted by M.Mohandas among **beedi** claimed that their health problems were because of their occupation (Mohandas 1980). The beedi industry is one of the largest employers in the unorganized sector and the bulk of the work-force is made up of women and children.

Many occupation may not be hazardous in themselves but the environment makes them such. In many other cases, an intrinsically hazardous industry becomes more dangerous because of lack of precautions or because no care is taken of the surroundings.

Some occupations become hazardous because of working conditions and the working environment. For example, children work at their own or in the artisan's houses that are clark and ill-ventilated as their occupants cannot afford anything better (Burra 1986). Given the lack of precautions, the delicate nature of children and their long hours of work, their eyesight is damaged in gem-polishing, diamond-cutting, carpet-weaving, zari work (gold thread embroidery), etc. (Jani 1986; Juyal 1985; and Khan 1987). The posture in which they sit for long hours while weaving carpets causes postural deformities and spinal problems (Boudhiba 1981). Had the working conditions been ideal, perhaps some of these hazards could have been eliminated or their impact reduced. But the piece-rate system, in which payment depends on the output at abysmally low rates, generates extraordinary pressure on the child to work for periods of time which are beyond his or her physical capacities (Burra 1988; 1986). In turn, this intensifies the hazards.

Many other jobs may be in what is considered a non-hazardous environment for adults but the situation of a child worker makes them hazardous. Occupations like domestic work, working in dhabas (roadside eating places), selling newspapers, etc. may be safe for adults, but the fact that children are at the mercy of the employer and do not have the support of their parents or anyone else puts them in a very poor bargaining position and consequently in a hazardous situation. Recently a 15-year-old boy was set ablaze by his employer, a factory owner because he asked for leave to visit his home in Bihar. He died of burn injuries (The Pioneer, 8 April 1994, The Times of India, 8 April 1994).

There are differing views on whether working in dhabas or as domestic servants is hazardous work or not. A survey in Bombay conducted by Usha Naidu, showed that working children were better off than non-working children in these two sectors. This analysis was based on height and weight measurements and working children were found to have an edge over non-working children. The explanation proffered was that working children were given food on the premises. While this may well be true, often children are given the left-over from the plates of clients. But there is another side of the picture, the grim reality of which makes the child very vulnerable.

A large number of children working in the dhabas and as domestic servants live on the footpaths or on their employer's premises. By virtue of being children, they are at the mercy of their irate customers and employers. Often they are vulnerable and fall prey to the anti-social elements of the urban jungle (Ganguly 1984; Rai 1984; and Pillai 1985).

Children are also sexually abused and made to pimp for the under world of thugs and gangsters that people the more sleazy and shadowy portions of the city. Sudhindra Shukla writes about the exploitation of the dhaba boys that leads not merely to physical but also to mental torture. Says Shukla:

It was a small, dark, dingy cafe or dhaba as it is known in Delhi. A grimy, peaky boy, ill-clad barely twelve years old, was handing out cups of tea to a dozen odd customers in the shop. I, too, was there. Balancing several cups in his two small hands this small boy was hurrying to serve the yelling customers, when a man rushing into the dhaba dived towards the wash basin, bumping into the boy and upsetting the tea cups. The tea spilled and the man's clothes were stained, so was his temper. He lashed out at the boy slapping him hard, leaving him in a trance (Shukla 1984).

The story related by Shukla is by no means unusual. Children interviewed by me in the Aligarh cbservation Home said they were severely beaten up by their employers for breakage of crockery. It was quite common for children to slip on wet floors of the dhabas carrying heavy loads of food and tea, thus not only incurring the wrath of the customers but also losing their wages till they had paid for the breakage.

Another factor that makes working in dhabas unsafe for children is that many of these tea-stalls or roadside hotels become gambling dens at night. The child worker who may be serving tea in the daytime is often made to carry bottles of liquor or peddle drugs among the clients at night (Anklesaria 1984).

Many children who work in dhabas live on the premises because they have either run away form home or have been sold by middle-men to the employers. They are at the mercy of the employer who often pushes them beyond their physical capacity (Singh et al 1980). This exploitation often includes sexual abuse. Dhabas owners very rarely employ slum children because these children are not available round the clock. Says Shukla:

A few days ago I chanced to meet such boys working in cafes of Bombay ...(They said) that many had to succumb or submit forcefully to sodomy, victimized either by the proprietors, the senior boys or the local goondas. All they say is kya karega saab, naukri karneka bai, seth log ka baat nahi manega to naukri to jayega, phir bahut maar bhi khane ko milega (What to do sahib, have to work. If we do not obey the bosses, we will not only lose our jobs but will be given the beating of our lives) (Shukla 1984).

Amit Sengupta, writing about working children, says:

In Old Delhi, Jama Masjid, Chandni Chowk, Ghanta Ghar and Paharganj I met children and adults who said there are many among those who rule the pavements, shops, dhabas and mohallas in these places who can rape children, sodomize them, and leave them in the grip disease (Sengupta 1985).

In the same way, children workings as domestic servants face very great hardships. Young boys of seven and eight years are often seen at five at in the morning walking the employer's dog or buying milk. Many of these children work from dawn to late at night, cooking, cleaning, washing and running errands. They are often not given adequate food and, if caught eating what they are not given, are subject to corporal punishment. Not only are they severely punished for mistakes but often accused of theft when the employer has merely misplaced his things (Boudhiba 1980; Ratnani 1985; and Indian Express, 22 February 1988). They sometimes end up with police records. It is this vulnerability which makes the working of children as dhaba boys or as domestic servants hazardous.

Health hazards are obviously of varying kinds. Horror stories abound and there is no saying that children in domestic, and dhaba jobs are better off than those in rag-picking or children working in unregulated workshops and factories. The degree of the hazard varies. In some cases, the hazard is obvious and in others it is insidious. In March 1994, I met ten-year old Rama Rao who had been beaten black and blue by his employer, the wife of an Air Force Officer, ostensibly for eating chocolates. When I saw him, he could not open his eyes and his head was misshapen. She had branded him with tongs. Rama Rao used to get up at 5.30 a.m. to fill water, sweep and swab the house, wash the utensils, fetch and carry. He was allowed to go bed only late at night. Rama Rao's employer had bought him for Rs. 600 from his parents. Whenever the employer beat him, she would turn the T.V. on loud so that neighbors would not hear his screams. Rama Rao was finally rescued by the neighbors and kept in safe custody by an NGO. He now goes to school. He was physically abused as a child at home so he did not want to go back to his parents. (The Times of India, 5 March 1994) Article 24 of the Indian Constitution, which is a fundamental right, states clearly that children below the age of fourteen years will not be allowed to work in any hazardous employment. But till such time as the word hazardous is not defined, children in many sectors will not even come under the purview of the law.

The classification of health hazards suggested above makes it clear that we cannot club together all categories of working children. The Government of India has taken the view that since children work on account of poverty and since governmental resources cannot match the magnitude of the problem, at the very least, children should not be permitted to work in hazardous occupation. But what has the government done about this? A look at the Status Report on Child Labour prepared by the National Institute of Occupational Health (NIOH) at Ahmedabad for the Child Labour Technical Advisory Committee (CLTAC) is revealing. Its major finding is that there is inadequate information about the health hazards working children face. The NIOH itself has investigated the slate pencil industry and it is reported that there are no epidemiological studies for other child labour concentration areas. The Status Report has not even put together all the data available in the form of newspaper and magazine articles and reports prepared at the behest of the Union Labour Ministry.

Regarding the glass industry, the Report has this to say:

In this industry there is a serious risk of physical injury, burn hazard, and exposure to silica containing dust. According to an NIOH study report (NIOH 1983-4) there was prevalence of 4.76per cent silicosis cases among eighty-four workers studied in the batch house of a glass sheet factory. On the other hand an ITRC study at Ferozabad (ITRC-1984) could not detect any silicosis cases. Hence, well planned and quickly executed studies at Ferozabad are needed before taking any action (Ramaswamy et. al. 1987).

Yet the Union Labour Minister himself along with some members of Parliament had personally raided factories in Firozabad and had found that some children were badly burnt and some others had even lost an eye (Amar Ujala 1987). Moreover, the glass industry has been thoroughly researched and an impassioned documentary has been made on the subject by film-maker, Meera Dewan. The authors of the Report seem to be blissfully unaware of all this work on the glass industry. Even if the Report was based on inadequate homework, it would have been in the fitness of things for the CLTAC to have sent teams of doctors and others to observe how the lives of children are quietly burning themselves out in the glass factories of Firozabad.

It is this insouciance and casual attitude that allows the Report to say about electroplating operations (commonly used in the lock industry of Aligarh and the brass ware industry of Moradabad). In these, cyanide solutions are handled. Hence, there is a necessity for regulating the conditions (Ramaswamy et. al. 1987).

Shouldn't children be banned from working with potassium cyanide, a deadly chemical, into a solution of which they dip their hands for the better part of a ten hour day, in the lock industry, for example? The lack of attention to work done in the past is reflected in the recommendations that more studies on the glass and brass ware industries are warranted. It is overlooked that these industries were banned, presumably for good reasons, by the U.P. state government under the Employment of Children Act, 1983.

The CLTAC has met in a perfunctory way and come up with piece-meal recommendations. One hopes that the CLTAC will visit the child labour concentration areas and sieve more thoroughly the evidence available in so many published articles and reports. The reports of the Children's Employment Commission and the Public Health Commission in England in the nineteenth century provoked considerable public debate for the wealth of data they made available on hazards to children, which ultimately led to the reform movement to end child labour in England. Will the CLTAC take the cue and grasp the opportunity to bring to light the horrific conditions under which children work and live in so many parts of the country?

8

Abolition of Child Labour
ILO Policy and its Implications

A. ILO Policy : A summer

1. The foundations of the International Labour Organizations' policy on child labour are set out in the Preamble of the Constitution, the Declaration of Philadelphia and relevant international labour standards, as well as in resolution adopted by the International Labour Conference and in decisions taken by the ILO Governing Body.

2. The fundamental objective of ILO policy in this mater is the abolition of child labour. The International Labour Organization set this as the goal in the very year of its creation, by adopting Convention No. 5, prohibiting work done by children less than 14 years of age in industrial undertakings. Sectoral Conventions and Recommendations on the minimum age for admission to employment which were adopted after 1919 (employment at sea, agriculture, trimmers and stokers,

non-industrial employment, industry, as did the Minimum Age Convention (No. 138) and Recommendations (No. 146), 1973. The International Labour Conference, in the preamble of Convention NO. 138, considered that "the time has come to establish a general instrument on the subject, which would gradually replace the existing ones applicable to limited economic sectors, with a view to achieving the total abolition of child labour."

3. The emphasis placed by 'International labour standards on the abolition of child labour attests to the conviction of the ILO's constituents that childhood is a period of life which should be consecrated not to work but to education and development; that child labour, by its nature or because of the conditions in which it is undertaken, often, jeopardizes children's possibilities of becoming productive adults, able to take their place in the community, and finally that child labour is not inevitable and that progress towards its reduction and even its elimination is possible when the political will to fight it exists.

4. This conviction is especially reflected in Convention No. 138 which requires member States to pursue a national policy designed to ensure the effective abolition of child labour, to set a minimum age for admission to employment or work and raise this progressively to a level consistent with the fullest physical and mental development of young people. This minimum age must not be less than the age of completion of compulsory schooling and, in any case, not less than 15 years. It should be noted that Convention No. 138 applies to work done by children both for another person (wage employment) and on their own behalf (self-employment).

5. Convention No. 138 is flexible instrument. This flexibility is illustrated by provision which:

(a) permit employment or work by children on light work from 13 years of age;

(b) allow for lower minimum ages (14 years in general

and 12 years for light work) in the case of countries whose economy and education facilities are insufficiently developed (for as long as this situation lasts);

(c) permit exclusion from the Convention's application of limited categories of employment or work in respect of which special and substantial problems of application arise (for as these problem exist);

(d) authorize member States whose economy and administrative facilities are insufficiently developed to initially limit the scope of application of the Convention, provided that it should be applicable as a minimum to: mining and quarrying; manufacturing; construction; electricity, gas and water; sanitary services; transport, storage and communication; and plantations and other agricultural under-taking mainly producing for commercial purpose.

6. Convention No. 138 and especially Recommendation No. 146 also contain some provision concerning the protection of working children. It should be noted that:

(a) these provisions apply only in the following cases, which are provided for in the Convention: light work; limited categories of employment of work excluded because the application to them of the Convention would give rise to special and substantial problem; and branches of activity and types of enterprise excluded pursuant to the option granted to member States to initially limit the scope of application of the Convention;

(b) protection basically concerns conditions of work (remuneration; hours or work, rest and leave; social security; and occupational safety and health).

B. Implications for ILO Technical Cooperation Activities

7. In the field of child labour, as in the International Labour Organizations' other fields of action, the role of technical cooperation is to b ring national law and practice closer to the model set out in international labour standards, so as to

promote their application or their eventual ratification. All ILO field activities relating to child labour should therefore be in line with ILO policy on this subject.

8. ILO technical cooperation, to conform with relevant international labour standards, particularly Convention No. 138 and Recommendation No. 146, should aim primarily to promote and support action in ILO member States which contributes to the effective abolition of child labour. Protection of working children, especially in terms of improving their conditions of work, can constitute another objective of technical cooperation. Nonetheless, this second objective is of a transitional nature, in the sense that it is pursued in anticipation of a comprehensive applications of the prohibition of child labour.

9. It is generally recognize that the complete abolition of child labour will take a long time, in view of the deep-seated causes of such work, such as family poverty resulting from parents unemployment or underemployment, from their limited access to training and from weaknesses in the system of social protection; quantitative and qualitative deficiencies in the education system; and passivity or even resignation about the problem, in Third World countries. The role of ILO technical cooperation is thus to ensure that a real start is made towards abolition and, in particular, that the intolerable is no longer tolerated. To this end, it should focus especially on encouraging and supporting action aimed at eliminating child labour in the types of employment (forced labour or bonded labour, for example), in the industries (mines and glass works, for instance) and in the occupations (such as prostitution or sugar cane cutting) which are clearly dangerous, i.e., detrimental to the safety, health or morals of the children concerned. Such elimination should be sought even if child labour in these dangerous types or employment, industries or occupations is not formally prohibited by legislation. This is often the case, for example, in relation to types of home work which involve exposure to toxic substances, to the recycling of household waste in public garbage dump sites. Another priority should be the reduction of the

incidence of child labour amongst the youngest and therefore most vulnerable children (those less than 12 years old, the age at which primary schooling generally ceases).

10. As for the protection of working children, it is necessary to bear in mind that the principal objective of ILO action is to abolish child labour for those children who have not yet reached a specified age or who are doing work which is liable to endanger their health, safety or morals. The ILO should assist governments to develop. implement and evaluate activities aimed at improving the lot of child workers with this aim strictly in mind. While the ILO can make proposals to member States for defining and setting priorities to alleviate the situation of the millions of children who work in order to survive, such proposals will be consistent with he priority objective mentioned above, which has been established by the International Labour Conference, only to the extent that they are framed within an overall goal to abolish child labour. The principle criterion for evaluating these measures should be the extent to which they have enabled progress, even if only in a particular sector of activity or region, towards the abolition of child labour, by reducing the extent of it or mitigating its consequences for children's further development.

11. It is of the greatest importance, in technical cooperation activities with a secondary aim protecting or improving the lot of working children, not of legitimize what is prohibited by ILO standards. The content of such cooperation must, therefore, be reviewed carefully to ensure that activities in the field are compatible with ILO policy.

12. ILO technical cooperation should mainly be addressed to the ILO's natural partners (governments and employers and worker's organizations) and aim to involve them more in the struggle against child labour. It should also support the NGOs which are active in this field.

13. The primary aim of ILO technical cooperation should be to help governments to define and implement a national policy

for the effective abolition of child labour (to use the terminology of Article 1 of Convention No. 138). This policy, the content of which should be determined in close consultation with employer's and worker's organizations and with other interested groups, should include or be linked with three main types of measure:

(a) in the first place, measures aiming to put a stop urgently to the intolerable (the use of children in dangerous types of employment, industry or occupations, as well as the use of very young and therefore, particularly vulnerable children);

(b) secondly measures aimed at changing attitudes and behaviors about child labour;

(c) finally, measures which, without explicitly addressing child labour, attack its causes.

14. The measures described in clauses (a) and (b) of point 13 above lend themselves well to ILO technical cooperation activities. They include:

(a) Knowledge of the Problem: little is known about the extent and distribution (by branch of activity or type of occupation) of child workers, about the conditions in which these children work and about the effects of this work on their physical, intellectual, moral or social development. Because of this ignorance, most existing programmes of action have principally benefited the most visible or "appealing" child workers (such as street children), and have helped very little those children who work out of the public eye (in domestic service, agriculture, or small workshops, as traders in the urban informal sector, or in home work). It is particularly urgent to identify the most dangerous forms of child labour. Likewise, a critical evaluation should be undertaken urgently of measures at the national level to combat child labour, so as to identify gaps and promising lines of intervention;

(b) mobilization of public opinion around the issue of

child labour, especially by supporting pressure groups (human rights or children's rights committees, for example) in their efforts to keep a systematically of abuses, to make them public and to highlight the breaches of their responsibilities by the public authorities;

(c) informing and sensitizing the general public, and in particular the actor in the struggle against child labour (governments, employer's and worker's circles, NGOs and other pressure groups), using the data gathered under (a) above and making wide use of the mass media (press, radio and TV);

(d) education of children and of those responsible for them (parents and teachers) on children's rights as workers, on the long-term costs of child labour and the possible alternatives;

(e) training of the people involved in the struggle against child labour (government ministry staff, labour inspectors, trade unionists representatives of employer's organizations, NGOs leaders, etc.);

(f) review of protective legislation and better supervisions of its application: the substantial disappearance of child labour in the organized sector of the economy is mainly due to the existence of legislation prohibiting it. In many Third World countries there are gaps in legislation on child labour. Its scope does not include certain activities, occupations or enterprises (agriculture, home work, domestic services, small enterprises) in which child labour is very widespread and often performed in dangerous conditions. Further, where work by children has not been outlawed their conditions of employment are often unregulated. These deficiencies should be corrected. Likewise, labour inspection has frequently not fully lived up to its responsibilities as regards supervision of protective legislation. Measures are needed to reinforce its effectiveness.

(g) implementation of programme of action aimed at preventing child labour, at withdrawing children from dangerous working situations, at facilitating their access of education, apprenticeship and vocational training services, or at improving their conditions of work and life; evaluation of the results of these programmes; their adaptation in the light of this evaluation,and their application on a larger scale;

(h) creation of an institutional mechanism within government, with responsibility for setting the main policy priorities, for coordinating the activities of the various Ministries and state institutions for ensuring that the measures taken by the public sector and those of the private sector complement each other, and for giving financial and technical support to the programme of direct action referred to in clause (g) above.

15. The measures referred to in point 13(c) above include those which aim to foster economic growth, to ensure a more equitable distribution of national wealth and to enhance the performance of the education and training systems. Such measures contribute to an improvement in the economic situation of the poorest classes of the population and thus to a reduction in the economic necessity for needy families to make their children work. The ILO can contribute to their success by offering technical cooperation in the fields of employment and incomes, manpower training and social protection. In this regard, particular attention should be paid to ILO operational activities aimed at mitigating the negative social repercussions of structural adjustment policies, at promoting more balanced development between town and country (access of peasants of land, credit, improved, seeds and better production techniques, as well as provision of drinkable water and education and health services in rural areas), or at enhancing the productivity of the urban informal sector and the conditions of work and life of the workers in it.

16. At the international level, the ILO obviously has a leading role to assume in the struggle against child labour. Nonetheless, some of the action required to attack the underlying causes of child labour (poverty, insufficient economic

growth and deficiencies in the education system) is within the competence of other international organizations (IMF, world Bank, GATT, UNESCO). UNICEF, for its part, is concerned with working children, especially those living or working on the streets, in the framework of its programmes for children in particularly difficult circumstances. The UN's Human Rights Commission has a working group on modern forms of slavery, before which cases of forced labour or bonded labour are regularly exposed. The diversity of mandates for action in the struggle against child labour should, therefore, be reflected in strengthened cooperation between the ILO and these other organizations and, most importantly, by close collaboration with UNICEF.

9

Current Trends for Combating Child Labour

Introduction

Efforts are being made consistently at the global level as well as at the national level various international organizations as well as their members in their respective countries to curb the tendencies prevailing among the employers for employing child labour in order to earn maximum profit but unfortunately results obtained so far have proved to be far away from being satisfactory. The nature and gravity of this problem has started posing as a serious challenge to the whole society and it has made the man-kind to focus attention on this problem by devising various modes to be adopted collectively with the sole object of improving the fate of child labour. The child labour has been eliminated in most of the advanced countries of the world but on the contrary the position in the context of child labour has deteriorated to a great extent in developing countries. This has been mainly due to the fact that poverty is the basic reason for promoting child labour and poverty is more rampant in developing countries due to financial constraints involved therein and gravity of this problem has assumed serious dimensions in terms of excessive exploitation of the of the child labour by their respective employers. Various international organization and agencies including International Labour Organization have started framing policies and action plans to tackle this problem considering it to be a serious threat to the whole society. International Labour Organization has taken a lead by formulating an International Programme on the Elimination of Child Labour which is an action programme to protect working children and to combat and eliminate child labour. The presumption of International Labour Organization has been that the children can not wait because they have but one opportunity for growth and development and they have the right to childhood.

Role of I.L.O. for Combating Child Labour - An Introspect

A cursory glance in the context of role of International Labour Organization for combating the child labour goes to establish in a convincing manner that the concerned recommendation have not been ratified and enforced in an effective manner by the member countries, particularly, the developing one. The scope of national provisions often fall short of providing complete coverage or in other words omit persons working otherwise than under a contract of employment and thereby exclude categories of work from the coverage of the legislation by excluding branches of certain economic activities from its purview. At the same time it has been observed which children may not work also varies considerably from country to country due to the fact that some countries only specify minimum age of employment for certain sectors while some way or another to the completion of compulsory schooling. In spite of the fact which approach has been chosen, it has been an essential factor that measures adopted in this regard might be expected to cover wherever possible all forms of work of employment. The aforesaid approach necessitates the adoption of flexible policy with regard to child labour so that requisite variations in approach might be adopted in consonance with the peculiar local conditions prevailing in each area of the country as the case may be.

It is a well established fact that the International Labour Organization has played a laudable role since its inception in the year 1919 for the abolition of the child labour. In this regard it might be brought out that Convention No. 5, of the I.L.O. explicitly provides for the prohibition in respect of employment of the children whose age might be less than 14 years in industrial undertakings.

Subsequently in the International Labour Conference held in the year 1973, an important convention, namely, Minimum Age Convention No. 138 and a Recommendation No. 146 were adopted regarding the child labour. In the preamble to the aforesaid Convention it was explicitly provided that the time had come to establish a general instrument on the subject, which would gradually replace the existing policies in this regard applicable to limited areas of employment, with an ultimate object to achieve the total abolition of the child labour. Under this convention member States of the I.L.O. were expected to pursue a national policy designed to ensure the effective abolition of the child labour, if possible, otherwise to prescribe a minimum age for the employment of children so as to ensure that physical and mental development of working children was not retarded in any manner and this age, as far as possible, should be correlated with the age of completion of compulsory schooling and in no case it should be less than 15 years. This convention also provided that the scope of concerned national policy would extend to children employed by the employer on wage basis as well as to the children having self-employment as a member of the family doing their own business. Keeping in view basic requisites necessitating flexibility in the national policy suited to the prevailing local conditions, it was also explicitly provided that age of employment for the children could be reduced to 13 years in case they might be required to do light work and minimum prescribed age was reduced even to 12 years for economic conditions compelled the poor parents to get employed their children in order to overcome conditions of starvation.

Recommendation No. 146 dealing with the child labour also provided for the protection of working children. Protection extended to the child labour under this recommendation has been mainly concerned with the conditions of work viz., and occupational safety and health.

ILO Technical Conventions and Implementation Process

International Labour Organization in the field of child labour has extended technical cooperation to the member States in order to enable them to frame their national policies in consonance with the International Labour Standards propounded by it so as to ensure effective implementation as well as eventual ratification by all member States. On the basis of the experience gained so far it has been fully established that the complete abolition of the child labour is a complicated task which is going to be a long term process so this programme has to be carried out in a systematic manner as well as in various phases. As a short term policy immediate action is needed to abolish child labour in hazardous employments, namely, mines, glass works, chemicals and pharmaceuticals industries. It has been increasingly realized that special attention is required to be given to such dangerous types of employments which are not explicitly prohibited by statutory enactments in vogue for the purpose of prohibition of child labour such as family employments which may involve exposure of small children to toxic substances, as in the case of farming which may necessitate the use of pesticides and insecticides as well as recycling of household waste and garbage including cow-dung for producing gas. These household activities result in undue exposure of small and delicate children to hazards having injurious impact on their health.

Recent activities resorted to solve the problem of child labour by the International Labour Organization highlight its crucial and significant role. It is being felt that the root causes of child labour manly include poverty, insufficient economic growth and deficiency in the education system and in this regard concerned International Organization, namely, International Monetary Fund, World Bank, GATT, UNESCO, UNICEF could play a significant role to cope up with the aforesaid deficiencies in order to regulate the problem of child labour instantly and to eliminate the child labour ultimately. In this Context it has been quite appropriately observed in the context of problem pertaining to child labour as under :

"The diversity of mandates for action in the struggle against child labour should, therefore, be reflected in strengthened cooperation between the ILO and these other organization and most importantly, by close collaboration with UNICEF."

In this context the role of the UNICEF is quite akin to the role of International Labour Organization for elimination of child labour in the sense that UNICEF is also concerned with working children specially those living or working on the streets and the frame work of its programme provide for children in particularly difficult circumstances.

Keeping in view intricacies and complications involved in the problem pertaining to the child labour, it is quite evident that no International Organization for children or concerned agencies could so far successfully solve the problem of child labour, so is imperative that International Labour Organization along with all other International Organization as discussed above should formulate their policies in a well planned and coordinated manner and implementation process should also entail requisite cooperation on their part in order to accomplish the desired goal of elimination of child labour, particularly, in developing countries. For this purpose funding of the action programme would be the first factor to be taken care of by the advanced countries on the same pattern as that of Germany which has taken a lead by providing requisite funds to the International Labour Organization for initiating the programme pertaining to elimination of child labour in developing countries in various phases.

International Programme for Elimination of Child Labour

The problem of child labour has become the focus of attention throughout the world and has shown serious repurcusions particularly in developing countries including India. An urgent need is being felt to combat with this problem by devising suitable means in each country in consonance with the existing local conditions. It is being increasingly realized that the child labour continues to be a problem of multifarious dimensions and it has been highlighted by the International Labour Organization in their recent International Programme on the Elimination of Child Labour that the number of the children working, and the scale of their suffering increases year by year and millions of the children are working, many in servitude and under hazardous conditions. This crisis existed in past, is being felt today and seems to continue tomorrow. In fact it is a glaring example of abuse of human rights although unanimously condemned but at the same time universally practiced, as child labour. By any objective measure this issue should rank high on the global agenda but in practice it is surrounded by a wall of silence and perpetuated by ignorance. As per ILO estimates more than 18 per cent of children in the age group of 10 to 14 years are working in developing countries and at least 7 per cent of the children are employed in Latin America, 18 per cent in Asia and as high as 25 per cent in Africa. It has been explicitly established in unambiguous terms that this problem poses a serious threat to the basic cause of humanity and necessitates remedial measures on war footings. Two serious fronts of this problem of grave concern risks and an explosion of the number of child worker in the informal and unregulated sectors of economy, as a result of increasing migration, urbanization and industrialization. It is quite disappointing to find that few parents due to poverty and resultant starving conditions sell their children to the wealthy people and in turn, such children are forced to work under slave-like conditions and are virtually imprisoned behind closed doors as domestic servants or prostitutes. Some of them are required to do the hot, mind-numbing and strenuous labour in various employments viz., brick making, sugar-cane cutting, sweatshops, etc. Unfortunately, it is being totally ignored that the children get single opportunity for growth and development and they have the right to childhood. The employer might be in a position to make short-term perspective, it is bound to prove to be too much expensive for a country due to the fact that such working children are not only exposed to physical, intellectual and emotional damage, rather the society as a whole has to suffer irreparable loss in terms of the diminished value of human resources for future development.

Implementation Process for IPEC (International Programme for Elimination of Child Labour)

International Labour Organization has selected child labour as a theme for focus in the year 1992-93 and a broader and more concentrated programme has been launched by it which is funded by the substantial grant provided by the German Government. At the first instance six ILO member States have been selected on the basis of the request made by them for availing ILO's assistance as priority countries for action programme for child labor and these countries are, namely, Brazil, India, Indonesia, Kenya, Thailand and Turkey. In the next phase six additional countries chosen for the action plan are Bangladesh, Cameron, Egypt, Pakistan, the Philippines and the United Republic of Tanzania. These countries could be claimed to be the model countries in the sense that excessive poverty among the common masses has resulted in increased exploitation of child labour by their respective employers and these action programme are likely to improve their working and living conditions substantially by enabling them to get better wages as well as prohibiting their employment in hazardous avocations.

It has been increasingly realized that the problem pertaining to child labour is quite complicated and it is not possible to solve it immediately by adopting a magic formulae. The gravity of the problem pertaining to child labour has variable dimensions in each country in terms of nature and degree of exploitation thereby providing varying scope for the action programme and consequently flexibility for selective operation in each action programme intended to be launched in each region or the country. International Labour Organization has formulated certain basic procedural rules and policies on the basis of which Memorandum of Understanding is executed between ILO and participating countries. In order to ensure effective implementation of action programme a programme Steering Committee comprising of one representative each of ILO, donor country, together with one representative of Brazil, India, Kenya are to be nominated by the Director General of ILO while the representatives of the other participating countries are to be invited as the observers. Members expected to play advisory role include a representative of ILO International Project on Child Labour and representatives of UNICEF and UNESCO. The main task to be performed by the Steering Committee mainly include setting of priorities, the approval of a biennial programme and budget; and the review of programme activities. The Programme Manager is expected to develop and implement strategies for a world-wide movement against child labour. Under the general supervision of ILO Management. The immediate objectives of these programmes are to ensure enhanced capability of ILO constituents as well as non-governmental organizations for the purpose of designing, implementing an devaluating policies and programmes for ensuring elimination of child labour and the protection of working children.

Target Groups for the Intended International Programme for

Elimination of Child Labour

The International Labour Organization, keeping in view, the complexities and intricacies of the problem pertaining to the child labour as well as financial implications involved for Elimination of the Child Labour in various phases and it is intended to give priority to such areas of employment of the child labour in each country which are the worst affected one in terms of gravity of exploitation of the child labour by their employers. Accordingly the priority would be given to children working under hazardous conditions in factories, cottage industries and agriculture. Top priority has been intended to be given to such areas of employment where children have been working under forced labour conditions either in agriculture or in informal sectors of employment. Target groups are expected to cover children that are specially, vulnerable to excessive exploitation by the employers thereby creating adverse impact on the health of children of tender age below 12 years or girl child labour. The children working as well as living on the street without family support are also priority target groups of child labour.

United Nations Convention and the Right of the Child

Article 27 of the Convention makes it obligatory for the State to recognize the right of every child to have a standard of living which may ensure requisite physical mental, spiritual, moral and social development of each child. Article 28 of the Convention imposes liability on the State to recognize the right of the child to education and for that purpose it is expected on the part of each State to make primary education compulsory and it should be available to all children free of cost. The State is also expected to take measure to encourage regular attendance at school and the reduction of dropout rates. AT the same time under Article 32 obligation has been imposed on each member State to recognize the right of each child for being protected from economic exploitation and from doing work of hazardous nature which may prove to be harmful to the health of child or retard the physical, mental, spiritual, moral or social development of the child. In compliance of aforesaid requisite conditions and in consonance with other international instruments for the protection of children, it has made mandatory for the Member State to take requisite statutory, administrative and social measures for the purpose of effective implementation of aforesaid relevant provisions and thereby recognizing right of the children to get primary schooling and to enjoy proper working and living conditions at the place of employment.

The basic commitment incorporated in a Convention, namely, Minimum Wage Convention of 1973, provided that each member State would pursue a national policy for abolishing the child labour and raise the minimum age for the employment of children to a level physical and mental development of young persons and in no case the minimum specified age should be less than the age of compulsory schooling which in any case could not be less than 15 years. But at the same time exemption has been provided to such countries whose economic and educational facilities are not properly developed and such countries could specify a minimum age of employment of 14 years. But it has to be ensured that the circumstances under which a child labour might be required to work are likely to adversely affect the health, safety, physical or intellectual development of young persons then in such cases in no situation minimum age of employment could be less than 18 years.

Similarly recommendation No. 145 of International Labour Conference concerning the minimum age for employment of children explicitly provided that in those employments wherein nature of the work provided to be done by the children would be likely to adversely affect the health, safety and moral of young persons or in other words nature of the work required to be done by the children is hazardous one, it would be essential to take into account relevant international standards relating to various matters viz., dangerous substance, dangers involved in process required to be utilized for carrying out manufacturing process including ionization or radiation, lifting of heavy weights or doing underground work, etc. It has also been made mandatory for the member States of the International Labour Organization to revise the list of hazardous establishments or occupations in the light of advancing scientific and technological knowledge. This recommendation also provides that the measures should be taken to ensure that the conditions in which children are required to work should be satisfactory to be exercised either by the employer or suitable and qualified persons on his behalf.

On evaluation of existing conditions pertaining to child labour in the context of International Conventions as well as commitments of various global organizations and their ratification by the member States, it might be opined that almost all developed countries and many developing countries have eliminated the child labour and children are provided compulsory and free education. The concerned member States have ensured that the employers should not employ children and the parents without regard to their poverty should send their children to school. The State has been made to recognise its basic duty of providing compulsory primary education to the children and thereby ensuring that the children should send their children to school. The State has been made to recognise its basic duty of providing compulsory primary education to the children and thereby ensuring that the children should not seek or continue any sort of employment. Unfortunately in some developing countries including India the primary education is not yet made compulsory and child labour in spite of statutory prohibitions continue to be a common phenomenon rather than exception. India, Pakistan, Bangladesh, Nepal are some of the developing countries in the Asian region where child labour has assumed alarming proportion and primary education is not compulsory in actual practice due to rampant poverty. On the other hand some of the other developing countries of Asia like China, South Korea and Taiwan have achieved high literacy rates by introducing compulsory education for the children in spite of low per capita income of common masses. Similarly many countries of African region viz., Botswane, Cameroons, Gambia, Ghana, Libya, Mauritious, Zambia, Zimbabwe, etc., have achieved higher literacy rate. All such factual position establishes that much disparity exists between international conventions and treaties with that of the existing position in reality in respect of child labour, therefore, it is high time that the concerned International bodies, in general and International Labour Organizations, in particular, should take effective and meaningful steps by implementing various programmes for ensuring improved working and living programmes for ensuring improved working and living conditions admissible to the child labour as a short term policy and total elimination of the child labour should be the ultimate target intended to be achieved.

Role of UNICEF and the Child Labour

The UNICEF has played a significant role for improving the conditions of child labour and it has been a major funding agency for improving the lot of children in general and child labour, in particular, specially in developing countries. Recently a Child Labour Cell has been created in six participating countries as discussed above including India whose main function is to work as National Focal Agency for documentation, advocacy, creating public awareness and organizing various seminars as well as training programmes. For this purpose UNICEF has sanctioned $ 0.5 million under their master plan of operation for the child labour programme for the five-year period commencing from 1991 to 1995. Two projects have been implemented on the child labour, namely, child Labour Action and Support Programme and IPEC Programme as discussed above.

Coordinated Efforts of International Organization and the Child Labour

International Labour Organization, UNICEF and

UNESCO have been making efforts in a coordinated and well planned manner to combat with the problem of child labour and for that purpose various programmes have been formulated and imposed, in furtherance of this objective these bodies organized, a five days Asian Regional Seminar on the subject 'Child Labour with Education and Enforcement of Legislation' which was held in New Delhi from 5th Feb., to 9th Feb, 1991 wherein a grave concern was expressed on the increasing number of child workers, particularly, in Third World Countries. The child workers, participating in this programme highlighted the fact that the concerned International Organization have jointly taken a decision to focus attention on priority basis to the problem of child labour and have taken up the basic programme for the elimination of child labour as a major theme of the integrated and concentrated action for the next five years, namely from 1991 to 1995. It was also pointed out that approximately 88 million children in the age group of 10 to 14 years were believed to be working in the whole world out of which atleast 67 million were estimated to be in Asian Region.

Feasibility for Elimination of Child Labour

It would not be improper to state that in case these International Organization who have under taken the challenging task to implement their plans, policies and programmes in a righteous manner, it would be possible to solve the problem which has so far posed as a serious threat and challenge to the whole world, particularly, in the context of developing countries where working and living conditions for the child labour are deteriorating day by day more particularly, in Asian and African region. The Programme of eliminating the child labour introduced at the first instance in six participating countries including India by the International Labour Organization is likely to show the positive results in terms of reducing the number of the child labour at the first instance and subsequently in phases when such programmes shall be introduced in six more participating countries with the financial assistance provided by the advanced countries like Germany, United States of America, Japan and other European Countries, it might be feasible to ultimately eliminate the child labour from almost all the developing countries. It may be pertinently pointed out that poverty and financial constraints faced by the parent of the children in most of the case compel them to get employed their children in order to overcome starving conditions. If requisite measures are taken such children by these International Organization, most of the parents are likely to choose for schooling of their children rather than getting them employed for doing odd jobs. Under such conditions it could be possible for the State to make primary education and once this process is initiated in a gradual manner in various phases in most of the developing countries, a day will not be far off when the dream of eliminating the child labour may prove to be a truth thereby ensuring the proper physical, moral and intellectual growth and development of the children who could ultimately succeed to acquire high qualifications and professional expertise in various fields thereby contributing to the growth and prosperity of their country.

Recent Policies and Programmes for Regulating Child Labour In India

It has been fully established on the basis of available statistical data as referred above that India is one of the countries having largest number of child labour in whole Asia and the existing state of affairs regarding the child labour convincingly highlight the glaring reality that all statutory and non-statutory measures taken so far to combat the child labour by the International Agencies, the State as well as Non-Governmental Organization (NGOs) have proved to be futile one or in other words failed to yield the desired results. The existing position with regard to child labour makes the concerned quarters to give a serious thought to this problem of child labour by studying the basic causes and reasons for the resultant problem of child labour as well as devising suitable ways and means by formulating and implementing various planned policies and programmes in a well organized and systematic manner.

Most of the researchers on the subject of child labour have mainly focused their attention on the nature and gravity of the problem, mainly, the total strength of the child labour in different sectors of employment and the percentage of he child labour in rural and urban areas as well as in formal and informal employments engaging the child labour but very few have suggested modes for regulating or eliminating the child labour. Therefore, in order to find a meaningful solution for the problem of child labour it becomes imperative to study the problem on this proposed pattern, primarily focusing attention on the basic causes of the child labour and the framing of feasible programmes in the form of statutory and non-statutory measures for accomplishing the desired and non-statutory measures for accomplishing the desired goals of combating child labour.

In this context it has been quite appropriately observed by Ms Leela Dubey that it would be totally misleading to associate child labour India only with industrial development, rather establishment of certain kinds of new industries, the reorganization of many cottage industries and crafts on non-familial and commercial basis as well as capitalization of agriculture have expanded the scope for exploitation of child labour. At the same time it may be pertinent to highlight the glaring reality that the involvement of children in economic activities is not a recent phenomenon in India rather a large number of rural people continue to thrive at subsistence or even below subsistence level mainly due to inflexibility and lack of mobility among rural folks due to which they continue to work with particular traditional paternal trade being pursued by members of specific castes and community ethnic group. These factors have highlighted the need for a better understanding of Indian Social reality, fewer generalizations, greater conceptual clarity and methodogical refinement.

According to Dr. K.D.Gangrade the traditional attitudes not only have contributed to the incidence of child labour rather certain other factors viz., urbanization, migration, lack of school have also equally contributed for the increased child labour. In majority of the cases it has been observed that the parents do not send their children to school mainly due to poverty and on the contrary children are pursued to seek employment so that their income may supplement other-wise meager income of the family. In few cases the children are made to work on the presumption that their early employment would prove to be a sort of training for them thereby enabling them to get a suitable job by the time they are fully grown up rather than to remain unemployed after schooling during childhood period. Many a times due to disease or disability in many families delicate budget is upset and there may be no alternative but to send the children for work. In rural families especially the economics of using school age children for agricultural work weigh heavily against sending them to school. Due to all these considerations in many poor families the children are considered to be assets rather than being liability on the presumption that they are considered to be profit-making machines as they seek employment family. Even in rural areas children provide active help to their families by doing odd jobs at the family farm or even at house. They help parents in ploughing field, sowing seeds, guarding crops against birds and animals, grazing of cattles, providing fodder to animals at home and feed to birds like cocks, hens as well as their young offsprings. Harvesting of crops and accompanying the male members to the grain market for sale purpose. In case the children get employment in rural areas in unorganized sector of employment such as beedi-making, carpet weaving and other small scale cottage industries they are in a position to supplement the meager family income by their earnings inspite of the fact that they are exposed to excessive exploitation by their respective employers. Many families migrate from rural to urban areas in search of suitable jobs. In urban areas children get employed in Dhabas, tea stalls, provision stores, cycle and scooter repairing shops and in such establishments they are required to work which they are required to do in such employments has injurious and adverse impact on the health of the growing children due to which they do not attain normal height fail to and enjoy proper physique on attaining majority rather they become weak and pale suffering from many deformities e.g., weak eye-sight due to overstrain, tuberculosis due to lung infection particularly in case of children working in bidi-making industries, match, mica and other chemical manufacturing industries. Similar children engaged in carpet weaving industries suffer from spondolytis and other related diseases due to continuous sitting for weaving carpets with a bent at a particular angle of the body.

Ineffective Implementation of Existing Labour Legislation for Child Labour

An introspect in respect of statutory and non-statutory measures taken so far in order to regulate the problem of child labour proves beyond any doubt that the legislature has from time to time enacted plethora of legislations for extending requisite protection to the child labour and the recent legislation on the subject, namely Child Labour (Regulation and Abolition) Act, 1986 is a comprehensive legislation aimed to regulate the working and living conditions of the child labour. But no legislation could be in a position to accomplish the desired goals unless it is implemented in an effective manner in consonance with its object and purpose. In fact existing pattern is that there is law for every problem with which the State is frequently confronted with and same is the position with regard to the child labour as discussed above but unfortunately very few legislations have been implemented effectively thereby providing requisite solution for the problem in question. In this context it has been quite appropriately observed by Professor Upendra Baxi that in India there has to be a law for every problem and accordingly many laws of India regulating adulteration, factory safety, child labour, minimum wages and bonded labour apparently give India the appearance of being a well-regulated Society whose State is devoted to the protection of the disabled, the poor and the powerless but in reality law has a symbolic value of setting norms but there is little concern with law as a means of individual compliance. Legislation and the arbitrary way in which laws are enforced or not enforced should be understood as a way in which the bureaucrats are engaged in a form to misuse their power and enhance income. Thus, factory acts and other legislation intended to regulate business are not enforced unless a businessman has incurred the displeasure of officials, in which case the law can be used as an instrument of punishment.

The aforesaid observation of Prof. Upendra Baxi brings forth in a righteous the existing position with regard to implementation process for statutory legislation. It would not be incorrect to say that effective implementation of statutory enactments mainly depend on the sincerity and desire of the bureaucrats to enforce it in strict terms, due to the reason many legislations including labour legislations have failed to accomplish the desired goals on account of the policy of senior officials not to displease big industrialists and to earn undue gains from the concerned quarters. The same has been the position with regard to some of the legislations applicable to unorganized labour, bonded labour and the child labour. In this regard, Prof. Upendra Baxi observed further as under:-

"...It is not that the Indian People as distinct from their governors, are unable to develop a strong commitment to legislation. It is rather that both the ruler and the ruled collectively feel that most legal rules do not set any genuine moral constraints to behavior motivated by strong personal or group interests. Rather, for the most part, rules are set to provide occasion for discretionary manipulation in a complex process of social interaction which is genuinely instrumental or result-oriented. Individual or group self-interest predominates over the value of following rules because they are rules, even if justified and justifiable ones."

The aforesaid observations in this regard highlight an

urgent need to evolve effective implementation process for existing labour legislations pertaining to the child labour, in general, and Child Labour (Prohibition and Regulation) Act, 1986, in particular so as to extend requisite legal protection to the child labour in order to ensure their proper physical and mental growth and development.

Role of the Trade Unions for Combating Child Labour

A cursory glance over the Trade Activities in organized and unorganized sector proves beyond a reasonable doubt that only a scanty role has been played by these Trade Unions Leaders of India have occasionally expressed their opinion against child labour but they have not so far played any meaningful role for compelling the Government to enforce Child Labour laws in a desired manner for preventing their exploitation by their respective employers. Although it has been observed that in many developed as well as developing countries of the world the respective trade unions have played a meaningful role for protecting the interest of the child labour but in India trade unions have not so far tried to organize any effective programme against the poor implementation of statutory enactments relating to the child labour. One of the basic reasons for existing state of affairs in respect of negative role of implementation machinery and indifferent attitude of the Trade Unions has been that children are mostly employed in cottage industries, small scale industries, small shops and business establishments, dhabas, restaurants or in domestic employments and due to the informal nature of such employments it is not feasible for the trade union leaders to organize employees working in such areas of employments and impose requisite pressure on the State for ensuring effective implementation of the existing legislation relating to the child labour. A general trend noticed in such employments has been that at the first instance parents personally get employment in such informal areas of employment and subsequently they get employed their children in such employments. Due to this reason a sort of pressure in the form of obligation of the employer continues to operate in their mind due to which they are not in a position to offer any resistance or express any resentment against the employer despite of having full knowledge of exploitation of their children by having employers at the place of employment. In this regard position in some other countries including the developing countries is quite different as many a time trade union leaders have expressed their displeasure and resentment for the exploitation of the children by the owners of sweatshops and other small scale business enterprises.

Process of Exploitation of Child Labour

As observed by Dr. Walter Fernandes that it is well accepted fact that the highest incidence of child labour is in agrarian sector and next to it is the unorganized and service sector of employment comprising of cottage industries, handicrafts and handloom works, small scale industries manufacturing machine parts, wires, switches, tanning, stitching, dyeing as well as shops and commercial establishments particularly small hotels, wayside dhabas which engage small children for providing service to the customers. Comparatively percentage of child labor is lowest in organized sector where they work in food products, wood and wood products, cotton and textiles and chemicals industries, as well as non-metallic mineral pro-ducts, steel industries and plantations. Recently another category of child labour has appeared on the scene due to greater unemployment, as observed by Dr. Prom. S.Vashistha, among the literate youth and persons with some literacy skills take over these trades in the informal sector thus relegating children from the poorer section to the less paid, more strenuous and lower status jobs. All these factors establish that instead of improvement in the living and working conditions of the child labour degree of their exploitation is increasing day by day.

The term 'Child Labour' is a multidimensional and generic term which includes within its purview several categories of workers. Strictly speaking there is distinction between the term child labour and child worker the former works on full time basis in lieu of wages payable after regular interval, child worker on the other hand often attends school regularly and during spare time at home he or she, either assists their parents in domestic work or agricultural pursuits or some other work done by the family and under these circumstances his involvement is on part-time basis. According to Walter Fernandes child labour is an 'intolerable evil' or a harsh reality' or a multi pronged serious problem affecting their lives of an extremely large number of children in an undeveloped country. It could be assumed that the children who thus become commodities in the economy where their services are extracted beyond their capacities, and invariably belong to social groups that are victims of injustice in other spheres too. Due to poverty and other similar reasons children are exposed to excessive exploitation by the employer without inhibitions and limitations and something due to which they are exposed to inhuman treatment, namely, sexual exploitation, doing work even during illness. In fact child labour may be exposed to working hazards in two forms, in one situation the occupation may not be hazardous in itself but proves to be dangerous both for the physical and emotional growth of the child particularly due to adverse working conditions and powerlooms, tea shops, dhabas and other small commercial establishments where there is darkness, improper ventilation, dampness, etc. and children are made to work continuously for twelve to fifteen hours without any rest-interval beyond their stamina and capacity. All these factors create adverse impact on the health as well as growth and development of the concerned children in spite of the fact that the working conditions do not involve any sort of hazard or danger. The other situation might be wherein the child labour may be required to work under hazardous process either due to the fact hazardous material such as poisonous chemicals or other material might be used in th plant or machinery or during the manufacturing process poisonous gases or vapours might be emitted or the child labour might be required to work on furnaces maintained at a temperature of 1500 to 1800 degree centigrate, thereby causing harm to the eyes, lungs and other vital organs of the child labour. In both types of work health of the child labour is adversely affected and they suffer in terms of physical as well as mental growth and development.

Working Hazards for the Child Labour

Children seek employment only under unavoidable and compelling reasons for the parents due to which they have to get them employed. It is very essential that reasonably safe conditions of working may be provided by the employers so that their health may not be adversely affected. But in reality it has been observed that they are made to work under adverse conditions which have injurious affect on their health as well as growth and development. Sometimes child workers are made to deal with poisonous materials or products at the place of work and at times during the continuance or work which may also include manufacturing process, wherein foul gases are emitted which have injurious effect on their eyes or lungs and retard their normal growth and development. In lungs and retard their normal growth and development. In this context it has been observed by Ms.Neera Burra that in some occupations workers might be allowed to come into contact with harmful substances like chemicals as in case of balloons, glass, match, fire works and lock industry and where fumes, dust or cotton fluff, etc., damage the lungs or any other organ of body and such occupations could be termed as intrinsically hazardous due to the reason that they could be hazardous for all types of workers children as well as adults but since the children still might be passing through the phase of growth and development so they fail to attain their full physical stature and there would to be an adverse and injurious effect on the health of the child labour. It has been established beyond any reasonable doubt that enough attention has not been paid to occupational diseases and most doctors might not be qualified enough to say whether disease native effective of poverty, malnutrition and unhygienic living conditions.

It has been quite unfortunate that all statutory and non-statutory measures taken so far in order to protect health and to ensure safety to child labour have failed to produce the desired results due to ineffective implementation machinery due to corruption on the part of inspection staff, political due to which child labour continue to suffer tremendously in terms of health, safety as well as growth and development.

Role of United Nations for Combating Child Labour in India

In the recent conference of United Nations on human rights held in Vienna the plight of the child labour was highlighted by bringing forth the reality that more than 80 million children employed by the employers in Indian Sub-continent have been leading a horrible life in Indian sub-continent and they could be found to be in servitude and to languish in bondage of their employers on account of being made to work for fourteen to sixteen hours a day in inhuman, unhygienic conditions as 'voiceless non-beings'. It was pointed out that about 55 million children were working as bonded labour mainly engaged in agriculture, mining, brick-kilns, construction work, activities of fishing, carpet weaving, fireworks, matches, glass moulding, bidi-making, gem-cutting and polishing, automobile workshops, metal-cutting and polishing work, electroplating, dyeing, washing and domestic service. In this conference it was observed that safeguards ad international conventions on child labor were being flouted in gross violation of human rights. In this context it was observed by the United Nations in its Conference held in Vienna that the children engaged for doing work are being excessively exploited by their employers mainly due to the fact that there are no statutory compulsions which operate effectively against the employer rather employers are generally found to dictate their terms to the child labour who do not enjoy good working conditions, prescribed working hours and holidays as well as fail to get adequate wages for the strenuous labour rendered by them for the production of goods on rendering material services. Such impression could be gathered from the aforesaid observations of the experts put forth in this regard, which are as under:-

"We purposely use the connotation 'Servitude' instead of 'Labour' in children's context Labour signifies the employee relationship in a society where a labourer has certain amount of bargaining power, freedom to organize and to go to litigation. Whereas 'servitude' implies a feudalistic master-servant relationship. A servant has no voice or freedom and hence reduced to sub-human condition."

It was also highlighted that 20 per cent of the children have been found to be working as child labour on account of being in the debt bondage either inherited from their grand parents or the parents which they could not pay off and their wages might be adjusted for paying of interest only and consequently they continue to work as child labour.

Keeping in view this process of exploitation of the child labour it was recommended in the conference on Human Rights that the United Nations must stop giving all financial support to projects which involve or perpetuate child labour and child servitude. These demands have been made by five non-governmental organizations of India, Pakistan and Bangladesh who have appealed to all importing countries that they should ban import of those goods which have been fully or partly made by the child labour with the object of discouraging the manufacture of products.

In this United Nations World Conference on Human Rights it was observed by the non-governmental organizations that Third World countries wherein the plight of the child labour has assumed serious dimensions such countries must appoint national commission on bonded labour including child Servitude which should be vested with statutory powers to identify, release and rehabilitate bonded labour including child labour. At the same time it was pointed out that the developing countries which were not having laws relating to abolition of child labour in hazardous employments and their regulation in other employments should be directed to enact legislation to combat child labour expeditiously.

It was highlighted in this Conference that many of the products exported by South Asian countries to other developed countries are generally made by these bonded child labour which manly include carpets, druggets, garments, leather goods, precious stones, brass item, glass products, marble, granite and surgical instruments, etc. In this context, it was observed by five Non-Governmental Organizations, namely, South Asia Coalition on Child Servitude and Bonded Labour, Liberation Front of India, Pakistan, Bonded Labour liberation Front, Nepal's INSEC and Bangladesh's Justice and Peace Commission, highlighting the appalling conditions of child labour in their countries such as the numerous conditions of mental toucher, beating, sexual harassment which reflected 'medieval-age slavery', it was urged by these organizations that despite constitutional guarantees, these organization that despite constitutional guarantees, legal safeguards and international conventions, 'exploitation of child labour and a violation of basic human rights' continued unabated. Therefore, it was proposed by these organizations that United Nations Human Rights Conference must stop all UN-aided support to projects that involve or perpetuate bonded or child labour. It was also appealed that the Conference should ask the Government of all importing countries to ban import of those goods which were fully or partially made by the children.

Impact of Social Action for Combating Child Labour

In a recent study of UNICEF in the context of unorganized sector, it has been quite appropriately pointed out that the owners of such industries intentionally and continuously hire children as they are well aware of the fact that by employing them they would be in a position to reduce the bargaining power of the adult workers as well as their number in their industries. Thus employers are in a position to exploit parents as well as the children. On the basis of experience gained so far the purpose of prohibiting and regulating employment of the child labour has produced encouraging results. In this recent study conducted like Germany have stopped buying Indian Carpets which are prepared by the child labour. In this context it has been recently highlighted that a trade mark is going to be introduced in Germany in terms of ensuring that the German buyers would purchase only those carpets which have been prepared without the help of child labour. This Trade Mark designated as 'Friendly Carpet Action' is expected do be popularized by the Indo-German Economic Project (IGEP). In this connection relevant instructions are being finalized by the concerned bodies of the Germany with the Ministry of Textiles, Carpet Export Promotion Varanasi. It is hopefully expected that the introduction of the Trade Mark is although likely to increase the prices of Indian employment of the child labour will be substantially reduced, with the passing of time export of hand knitted carpets is getting more and more acceptance by the foreign purchaser which is quite evident from the fact that nearly Rupees fifteen crores are being paid annually by the Germany for importing such introduced these carpets will be in much demand which are being prepared without the involvement of the child labour. In United States of America also there is repulsive attitude among the purchasers of the carpets made by the child labour. In this context the administration of United States is contemplating a ban on the products which involved child labour. The Trade Mark to be formulated is intended to simplify identification and provide a guarantee that the carpets have been prepared without child labour. Carpet producers at Varanasi have explicitly and in clear terms assured IGEP that the child labour would not be used in Carpet knotting. On the basis of such assurance given by these carpet manufacturers IGEP has also assured all possible support to them for their products in Germany once the Trade Mark is introduced. In European Countries since a long a tendency has been noticed that day by day an approach has been developing among the traders and purchasers of the

Carpets and other products prepared by the children to discard their consumption particularly those which involve child labour and are prepared by developing or poor countries of Asia and Africa. It is quite evident that this resentment which operated earlier in the form of Social action is gradually getting legal recognition in European countries. This movement which has invited attention of advanced countries is going to show positive results in terms of discouraging the employment of child labour and this process is expected to go a long way in terms of improving the lot of the children in developing countries of Asia and Africa, in general and in context of India, in particular.

Although the statutory measures provide for the abolition of child labour in hazardous establishments but in reality they are being made to work under the most hazardous working conditions in gross violation of express statutory provisions. Study conducted by the UNICEF has highlighted that the children are required to work with hazardous chemicals of highly dangerous properties like potassium cyanide, Tridum and phosphate during the electroplating process continuously for a long period which injuriously effect their health. As these children are not well acquainted with the dreadly properties of these chemicals so due to their careless handling quite frequently they even loose their life. The owner of these factories carry scant regard for the relevant provisions of the Factories Act, 1948 which are flouted by them in a gross manner thereby endangering the life of child labour. It has been claimed by UNICEF that is the largest producer of illiterates and child labourers.

All this relevant information brought out by the UNICEF could establish in clear terms that all statutory and non-statutory measures taken so far have just negligible impact in terms of improving the lot of child labour. Rather the gravity of the problem highlighted under this study imposes responsibility on the Government to provide solution for improving the horrifying state of the child labour by devising ways and means to tackle this problem which has assumed serious dimensions at international level and its impact is the cussed here in to attract and focus attention of the Government on the plight of the child labour.

Recent ILO Estimates Regarding Child Labour

The recent surveys regarding child labour brought out by the International Labour Organization highlighted the glaring reality that the number of child labour has exceeded 5 millions out of the total 15 million bonded labour working in India and it has been in sharp contrast to the figure of child labour only marginally exceeding 353,000 as reported by the National Sample Survey of the Government of India. The International Labour Organization in its survey focused attention on the atrocities against children by highlighting the fact that young children of even six years are made to work for a long duration of seventeen to eighteen hours. Some of the children work as bonded labour and in order to ensure that they may not run away they are beaten regularly and kept locked up day and night in sweetshops and they are tortured and sometimes even killed in order to create terror in their mind so that they may not try to abscond from the place of their bondage. According to reports of the ILO Committee of experts it was highlighted that several million Indian Children in the age group of 5 to 14 years are in chronic bondage in the field of agriculture. Other important areas of the employment where in millions of child labour have been working are brick-kiln, stone-quarry and construction industries. In diamond cutting industry also millions of children are found working. Other areas prone to employment of children are domestic employments wherein children work in slave like conditions. This is infact the problem of not only India rather it has assumed serious dimensions in countries like Pakistan, Thailand, Sudan, Haiti, Peru, Brazil, Mauritania and the Dominican Republic.

It is established that the problem pertaining to child labour has assumed seriousness to an alarming extent not only in India rather at international level particularly in the context of their exploitation in developing countries of Asia and Africa. It would not be an exaggeration to mention that India is leading in terms of engaging maximum number of child labour and permitting their exploitation by the respective employers to an intolerable extent. An attempt is to be made to take into account social as well as legal parameters of this problem with special reference to statutory enactments in vogue in India with regard to the child labour in order to find out the requisite ways and means to tackle this serious problem on an urgent basis. This would involve an in-depth study of various legislations on child labour with an object to find out deficiencies and lacunas involved in them with the support of relevant case on the subject in order to suggest suitable amendments required to be made in order to make such legislations more effective as a short term measure and to enact and enforce comprehensive legislation on child labour in order to control the existing situations, as a long term policy. An introspect will also be made in respect of proposal for introduction of compulsory education by the Government for the children upto the age of 14 to 15 years in order to eradicate child labour below the age of fifteen years.

10

Existing Conditions for Child Labour - A Comparative Introspect

Introduction

It has been brought out recently in a study conducted by International Labour Organization that the number of the children working as bonded labour has increased alarmingly and is approximately five millions and not only 335,000 as announced by the Government of India. The International Labour Organization has highlighted the reality that not only in India rather in Pakistan, Thailand, Sudan Haiti, Peru, Brazil, and Dominion Republic also, the Governments were confronted with serious problem relating to child labour as in these countries also, child labour was working as bonded labour akin to child slaves, being in the age group of six years to seventeen years and were compelled to work for seventeen to eighteen hours continuously. The bonded child labour are sexually abused, beaten up and are even killed if they try to escape from the custody of their master or the employer. According to the report of ILO Committee of experts several million children in India within the age group of five to fourteen years were in the chronic bondage in agriculture and at least one million in brick kiln, stone querry and construction carpet weaving and diamond cutting industries.

The findings of the International Labour Organization could highlighted the plight of the child labour not only in India rather in many other developing countries. The serious implications of this problem of aggravated nature which has spread its tentacles not only in India rather over most of the developing countries of the world needs to be tackled, in a systematic and planned manner by framing policies and programme by the concerned countries being confronted with this problem, in coordination with each other. In this regard the International labour Organization can play a meaningful role by framing revised conventions and recommendation regarding child labour which should provided for minimum standards to be adopted by all the countries. It has been observed that social action groups could play an effective and meaningful role, particularly in the industrialized countries at international level as well as national level by building up public opinion against the use of goods produced by child labour. Movement has already started by rejecting the carpets made by child labour in Third World Countries.

Latest Findings Regarding Child Labour in India

Recently a meaningful role is being played by the Centre of Concern for Child Labour by conducting useful surveys and revealing sensational details regarding child labour that the child labour is more concentrated in Traditional professions involving low technology viz., carpet weaving, lock making, bidi rolling, matches and fire work industry, stone quarries, mines, fishing, etc., According to them at least 44 million children have been working in various employments and some of them could be as young as seven years only. According to the survey conducted by the Centre of Concern for Child Labour the employment of children in non-formal sector has been increasing rapidly as compared to modern industries involving technology of advanced nature. Small scale industries, particularly, in rural areas like family based cottage industries, toys industries, domestic utensils producing employments, etc., engage more unorganized labour including their personal children.

Constitutional Commitments and the Child Labour

It may not be out of place of mention that the problem of child labour has been consistently posing serious threat to the State. It could be stated in the right perspective that although there had been lack of serious efforts on the part of the State which mainly includes the legislature and the administrative machinery under its control, but it would not be justified at all to say that no efforts have been made in this regard. A Cursory glance over the Constitution of India would reveal that few relevant provisions relating to child labour as well as child welfare have been incorporated in Part III and Part IV dealing with Fundamental Rights and Directives Principles of State Policy respectively. Under Part III it has been explicitly provided in Article 24 that the children below the age of 14 years could not be employed by the employers in any factory or mine and their employment has been absolutely prohibited in hazardous establishment. It is quite evident that Dr. B.R.Ambedkar and other framers of the Constitution were quite aware about the problem of child, labour and due to this reason a Fundamental Right in favour of children was incorporated by them in Article 24 and resultantly, the employers were totally prohibited from employing children below the age or fourteen years. In compliance with this Constitutional commitment provision for prohibition relating to employment of child labour below the age of 14 years and regulating the employment of child labour above 14 years were included in various labour legislation viz., the Factories Act, 1948; The Plantations Labour Act, 1951; The Mines Act, 1962; The Merchant Shipping Act, 1958; The Motor Transport Workers Act, 1961;The Apprentices Act, 1961; The Shops and (Commercial) Establishment Acts of Various States as well as Union Territories; The Bidi and Cigar Workers (Conditions of Employment) Act, 1966; etc. The aforesaid action on the part of Central and State Governments as well as Local Bodies could highlighted the will, desire and anxiety of the legislature to accomplish the task of prohibiting and regulating the child labour as per constitutional compulsion due to recognition of the Fundamental Rights by inserting relevant statutory provisions in various labour legislation regulating employment of workers in various areas of employments. It would not be out of place to mention that Article 23 of the Act also deals with child labour due to the reason that even if it provides for forced labour but children definitely constitute a substantial part of the labour force whose exploitation has been prohibited under Article 23 which provides in explicit terms that exploitation of the Working class as forced labour shall be an offense punishable in accordance with the relevant law which would mainly comprise of relevant provisions of aforesaid legislations as well as that of Child Labour (Regulation and Prohibition) Act, 1986. At the same time in order to prevent exploitation as well as the abuse of child labour relevant provisions have been included in part IV of the Constitution dealing with Directive Principles of State Policy. In this context it is explicitly and in a precise manner, provided in Article 39 clause (e) that the health and strength of not only the man and woman rather the children of tender age should not be abused by their employer and the State has been directed to frame the policies for ensuring them requisite protection in this regard. The intention of the framers of Constitution could be easily gathered that they were bothered about the working class, in general and women as well as children, in particular. In this regard a duty has been imposed on the State to see that the children may not be compelled to do arduous or hazardous jobs unsuited to their health and capacity so that their physical growth and mental development may not be retarded in any respect.

The State could perhaps have clear and definite assessment about the exploitation and abuse of the child labour by their employer and inability of the implementation and enforcement machinery, in order to control the existing situation as an amendment was introduced in Article 39 and new clause (f) was substituted which provided for giving requisite opportunities and facilities to the children in order to enable them to develop in a healthy manner by providing conducive atmosphere wherein they may be in a position to enjoy conditions of freedom and dignity. The State is directed to ensure that they should not be exploited for and due to their specific needs by the people, particularly, their employers in case they seek employment, by making to such children available material resources in abundance. At the same time moral values may be imbibed by the State in them so that the children may have moral strength to adopt the right path and to have moral strength to face the odd situation to which they may be exposed, with courage and patience.

The Supreme Court of India in case of M.C.Mehta vs State Tamil Nadu observed in this context that the spirit of the Constitution is that the children should not be employed in factories due to basic reason that the childhood being the formative period, proper growth and development of child, would take place only during this period, keeping in view, this basic aspect, the framers of the Constitution provided explicitly in Article 45 under Part IV of the Constitution of India dealing with Directive Principle of State Policy that free and unless they attain the age of 14 years. It had been observed by the Supreme Court in case of Democratic Rights vs Union of India (Asiad's Workers case) that the construction work was a hazardous employment and, therefore, no child below the age of 14 years could be employed in construction work. Even if it was contended on the part of employers that the minors accompanied male members of their families and such children as well as their parents emphatically requested and insisted for getting employed but this contention was not accepted by the Supreme Court on the ground that the employment of children below the age of 14 years was totally prohibited in hazardous employments as provided under Article 24 of Constitution of India. In this context it would also be relevant to highlighted the observation of the Supreme Court that it would not be possible to eradicate the child labour so long as poverty and destitution continued in the country, but inspite of that it would be essential the existing socio-economic conditions, it has to be conceded that it would not be possible to prohibit child labour in unconditional and absolute terms due to the fact that such move might not be socially and economically acceptable to large masses of people.

Due to this reason Article 24 of the Constitution of India prohibited employment of child labour only in factories, mines or other hazardous employments and permitted their employment in other professions and vocations. It was held by the Supreme Court that Construction work was hazardous employment and no child below the age of 14 years could, therefore, be allowed to be employed in construction work being prohibited under Article 24. This Constitutional prohibition must be enforced by the Central Government. The Supreme Court has observed in the right perspective that the employment of the small children below the age of 14 years has to be prohibited in hazardous employments and for that purpose it would be desirable on the part of the Government to take appropriate statutory and non-statutory measures. The Child Labour (Prohibition and Regulation) Act, 1986 has to be suitably amended and more establishments doing the work of hazardous nature and exposing children to dangerous work should also be included within the purview of the Act. For that purpose list of the hazardous establishments provided in the Act which expose child labour to any sort of danger should be included within the scope of the Act as the legislature did not include even the glass industry wherein the children are required to work near furnaces kept at 1400 C to 1800 C and the slate industry wherein children work under hazardous conditions. It has been observed by some experts that basic draw back is involved in the very object of the Act itself as it is intended to achieve two controversial goals viz., Prohibition and regulation of child labour but in actual practice it could concentrate either on prohibition or regulation of child labour for the purpose of reforming the life of working children but the author is personally of the view that he object of the Act is to prohibit in absolute terms employment of child labour in hazardous employments and to regulate their employment in all other professions or vocations. The Child Labour (Prohibition and Regulation) Act, 1986 has been enacted and enforced in order to overcome the lacunas and ambiguities involved in the Employment of Children Act, 1968, for that purpose this Act has been repealed by the recent legislation, namely, the Child Labour (Prohibition and Regulation) Act, 1986. Undoubtedly the present legislation is more comprehensive and meaningful but unfortunately it also suffers from few basic drawbacks. First of all, it may be pointed out that the scope of the Act is quite limited and the remedies available under it are quite few mainly due to the fact that unorganized labour has not been covered within its ambit or in other words continues to be outside the provision of the Act, consequently the benefit of the statutory protection is denied to the unorganized labour, in particular, the child labour. In this context it has been appropriately observed that child labour is absolutely legitimate as Government legislation on the subject still continues to help employers to get their work done at half of the amount otherwise payable to the adult workers by engaging the child labour which provides the employer same quality of work.

Poorly drafted legislations pertaining to the child labour provides a lever in the hands of the employer to engage the child labour by paying them meager wages and to evade the liability so incurred by claiming exemption under one or more ambiguous provisions of the concerned machinery encourages the employer to exploit the child labour.

The employer with the sole object of earning maximum profit engages the child labour fearlessly and evades its liability by passing a share of the profit to the concerned officials who consequently the concerned employers. This practice ultimately nullifies the whole impact of the statutory prohibition imposed against the employer. Population explosion has resulted in more poverty and unemployment due to which parents of the children under compulsion permit their children to seek employment in order to avoid starvation. This results in increased supply of the child labour as compared to the demand for the same Resultantly the poor parents continue to progress and pretend ignorance regarding the exploitation of their children in spite of having its full knowledge as they could by their employers. So increased employment of the child labour has become a common phenomenon and the statutory only a symbolic relevance. Due to the aforesaid reasons the Constitutional safeguards have lost their utility.

The provisions of Article 45 still continue to be a far cry due to the fact that economic compulsions of poor people have forced the children to seek any sort of employment available to them as increased unemployment has, generally, prevented them from seeking suitable employments thereby providing labour without having any regard to their health as well as growth and development. This problem has been in existence for the last so many years-exceeding even half a century but the attention of the Government could not be focused immediately particularly in terms of enactment and enforcement of appropriate Act. In this context it was recently brought to the notice of Supreme Court under public interest litigation by an advocate and social reformer M.C.Mehta thereby establishing that in reality the social-reformers and voluntary organization of child labor as well as for eradicating child labour in hazardous employments. The Supreme Court in case of M.C.Mehta vs State of Tamil Nadu held that the manufacturing process of matches and fireworks was hazardous one due to the fact that inspite of the best possible care and improved techniques fatal accidents used to occur in these establishments. The working conditions available to the workers, particularly, the child labour established that they not only involved health hazards in normal and routine course rather the nature of the manufacturing process involved therein was bound to adversely affect the health of the child labour thereby posing problems in terms of their growth and development. The exposure of children of tender age to such hazardous working conditions required to be given special attention. Hence it was observe by the Supreme Court that the employment of children within the premises of match factories for doing work directly connected with the manufacturing process upto final production of match sticks or fire works should not at all be permitted. At the same time it should be ensured that the child labour who might be in employment and need employment urgently due to poverty and other compelling needs should not be thrown on the road. Keeping in view all these factors, the Supreme Court opined that the children could, therefore, be employed in the process of packing but in order to avoid exposure of the children to hazardous conditions and consequential occurrence of accidents this work of packing should be done at a place which must be away from the place of manufacturing process of the factory or establishment. It was further emphatically put forth by workers were more suited to the work of sorting out manufactured products and to process such products for the purpose of packing rather than involving them in the manufacturing process itself which may expose them to hazardous working conditions.

National Policy on Child Labour

The Governmental has been making efforts consistently to protect the child labour by prohibiting their employment in absolute terms in hazardous employments as well as to regulate the employment of child labour in order to prevent their exploitation by the employer in other areas of employment by ensuring effective implementation of Child Labour (Prohibition and Regulation) Act, 1986. In order to accomplish this task in the year 1987, the Government of India announced three pronged National Policy on Child Labour aiming firstly to prevent exploitation of children as well as to ensure their suitable rehabilitation in case of their withdrawal from prohibited areas of employment. This policy was mainly intended to ensure effective and meaningful implementation of the Child Labour (Prohibition and Regulation) Act, 1986 and other relevant provisions of the labor legislation dealing with child labour under the legal action plan. Secondly to formulate and implement project based plan of welfare and development programme for the child labour which provided for 30,000 children in 10 projects in the first phase having a budget of 11 crores with object of rehabilitating these children after being withdrawn from prohibited areas of employment. The basic objective of the programme had been to improve the health, nutritional status, working conditions, qualifications and professional skill of the child labour. Regarding these programmes doubts have been expressed due to the fact that earlier programmes of the Government enforced for the purpose of providing welfare facilities to the working children in various districts of eastern Uttar Pradesh e.g., Sivakasi, Mirzapur, Bhadohi, Varanasi, etc., failed to provide good and encouraging results.

Implementation Process of Labour Legislation Relating to Child Labour

It is a well recognized and universally accepted fact that the basic reasons for the exploitation of child labour has been non-implementation of existing Labour could be put-forth for the existing disappointing state of affairs. Firstly, the concerned law is covered, under the category of 'Social Welfare Legislation' which is basically intended to change socio-economic structure of the society by enacting and enforcing with the existing needs of the common man. Legislations relating to child labour have been enacted in a piece-meal manner which enable the employer to commit their violation in a convenient manner, particularly, in connivance with the inspection staff. Comprehensive legislation for protecting the interest of child labour would not only remove the disparities involved rather could be effectively implemented by making reasonable rather than excessive efforts. This problem is being felt not only in India rather in most of the developing countries. In this context it had been quite appropriately highlighted in an ILO. study on child labor that although most of the developing countries have enacted adequate legislations on child labour but these statutory measures have failed to yield the desired result by ensuring prevention of exploitation of child labour. Broadly speaking child labour has persisted in a proportion which have been found to show nexus inversely to the nature and extent of economic development of society, country of region. The exploitation of child labour has been the outcome of complex and unchanging nature of the society not particularly in most of the developing countries rather in some of the developed countries as well. The basic reason could be assigned to the existing socio-economic conditions wherein children instead of being in a commanding position occupy unfortunately a demanding position due to which it could not be feasible for the children to negotiate with their employer regarding the condition of work which had been imposed on them in an unilateral manner by their employer and unfortunately there could be no trade unions of the child labour to defend them, consequently they could not have access to social security schemes. The great social advances working children. It could be easily understood that the poverty of people led to exploitation of their children as they could not afford to let their children loose their employment by confronting with their employers. Child labour continue to be unorganized one in most of the employments and the trade unions have failed to protect their interests. They are also generally deprived of social security benefits otherwise admissible to the industrial workers. All these factors cumulatively lead to their victimization by their employer thereby compelling them to work for meager in adverse working conditions operating against employers. In the context of operation and implementation of law relating to child labour, it was observed by Dr. S.N.Jain that the laws relating to child labour would be covered in the category of social policy legislation where the main task of law would be to play a leadership role to change the socio-economic structure of the society. The basic impediment with regard to implementation of child labour legislation, as pointed out by him, had been that the operation of child labour laws had demonstrated the difficulties of the law in playing this leadership role, particularly when isolated law could be passed to deal with particular subject within the basic structural-wise status quo society as brought forth predominantly by various studies a conducted on child labour so far on this subject. For enacting a social policy law, it should be accompanied by other measures, namely, enactments of other laws, machinery for the enforcement of laws other social and economic welfare measures which might necessitate change in the entire socio-economic environment.

It would not be improper to mention that comprehensive legislation should be enacted which may be implemented with the aid of non-statutory measures in the form of socio-economic measures having focus of operation on the aspect of improving lot of child labour.

Discrepancy in Terms of Statutory Definition of Child Labour

The statutory definition of 'Child Labour' provided under various legislations lacks uniformity in the sense that there is no uniformity with regard to age for being considered to be others it is fourteen years. Although the age so prescribed under concerned labour legislation has direct nexus with the nature of the work and the degree of the risk involved therein but even in this context as well, it lacks uniformity and consequently it has become a root cause of controversy and confusion. The definition of child labour also varies from one State to that of other State, in the sense that in Madhya Pradesh, Uttar Pradesh and Punjab, a child would mean and include a person under sixteen years age, while in Gujarat and West Bengal a person under eighteen years, in a State of Andhra Pradesh a child means a person of fourteen years or less than that under the Children's Act, 1960 applicable to Union Territories a child is defined a boy under sixteen years evolve uniform definition of child which may incorporate relevant factors pertaining to professional risks and hazards of each profession. Child labour in organized Sector comparatively enjoys legal protection due to statutory restrictions in force in various arena of employment but they have to work under miserable conditions in unorganized sector due to the fact that most of the vocations or employments do not fall within the purview of statutory restrictions in vogue in organized sector of employment. Although Minimum Wages Act, 1948 covers within its purview child labour working in unorganized sector but in reality its effect is just negligible because enforcement of Minimum Wages Act in a requisite manner in the unorganized sector.

Basic Reasons of Exploitation of Child Labour

One of the basic reasons leading to exploitation of the child labour has been not only the inadequacy of statutory legislations to protect their interest rather their improper implementation. Shortage of staff mainly related to enforcement process as well as lack of sincerity on their part leads to existing plight of the child labour. Corruption on their part is another important factor which leads to negating the impact of statutory measures taken so far in order to improve the living and working conditions of the child labour.

It could not be justifiable and possible to ignore the statutory and non-statutory measures taken so far for the purpose of improving the existing disappointing condition of the child labour but certainly non-statutory measures taken by voluntary agencies, experts, non-Governmental Organizations and other concerned people tend to overweigh the statutory measures taken so far. This impression was gathered on the basis of recommendations and suggestions put forth by some of the well recognized personalities of India. On children's Day (14th November, 1992), it was observed by Justice P.N.Bhagwati, the former Chief Justice of India that national campaign against Child Labour was launched that day to mark the Children's Day. He could bring-forth that about 18 million children constitute a part of the labour-force out of 159 million child population in India and surprisingly he could highlight the fact that economic necessity is not the only reason that perpetuates the child labour. According to him the real reason was the objective of the industries to make more profit as children can be engaged for low-wages and can be made to work for long hours without any protest on their part mainly due to the submissive nature of the children. He could quite appropriately quote the experience of African Countries where the spread of compulsory education has enabled to a large extent in eradicating child labour. He was of the view that compulsory education of children is bound to produce positive results in India as well.

Another well known expert Dr.Aramaity Desai, who is Principal Bombay-based Tate Institute of Social Sciences (TISS) was on the other hand of the view that poverty was the sole reason for the continuance of child labour. She could also highlighted another important aspect that child labour works against the interest of adult labour in the sense that children are available for work on low wages which not only leads to flouting of labour laws rather drives the adult labour out of the employment market as the child labour fulfills the need of the workers of the employers by substituting themselves in place of adult labour. She was also of the opinion that profit motive in Industry is the sole reason for employing child labour.

Proposed Remedial Measures for Child Labour

George Chirs of Terre Des Hommes (TDH) in furtherance of the campaign launched against the child labour proposed that it is urgently needed to abolish child labour should absolutely operate as long term policy. He also emphasized that effective measures should be taken to maximum hours of work for children, provision of nutrition, informal education and medicare at the work place by the employer. He observed that this November 1992, rather similar campaigns had been launched in various parts of the country. Another important personality Ms Alpa Vohra of well-recognised Non-Government Organization of Bombay, namely, YUVA said that the immediate objective of the campaign is to reinforce local and regional efforts towards the eradication of child labour. She could highlight that the campaign against child labour had the effective involvement and participation of sixty Non-governmental Organizations (NGOs) from 11 States of the whole country. This campaign was intended to reinforce local and regional efforts towards the eradication of child labour. Its object was also to win public support for the cause of eradication of child labour and to advocate the ratification by India of U.N.Convention on the Rights of the Child (1990) signed by 115 countries of the world. By this campaign, it was emphasized that compulsory education of the Children would make substantial difference in improving the lot of child labourers. By virtue of education, awakening is likely to be created among the child labour and consequently they can be expected to fight unitedly to prevent their exploitation as well as to ensure full development of their potential. As a pleasant surprise she could cite that the instances of child labour are the lowest, being only 1.9 per cent of the total children, in a State of Kerala which is mainly due to highest literacy rate of the State in the whole country. These observations go to establish in clear terms that the increased literacy among the poor working class in general and the children in particular is bound to provide an effective measure for regulating the problem of child labour due to the fact that literacy will create more awakening among them and they will fight in an organized manner against the employers and could prevent their exploitation by their employers and may be in a position to ensure ultimately payment of better remuneration and admissibility of good working conditions to the child labour at the place of their employment.

There is an urgent need to frame a scheme pertaining to the eradication of child labour in hazardous employments and regulating their employments in non-hazardous employments in a planned and systematic manner. For that purpose it is essential to invoke equal participation in an effective manner of Governmental statutory machinery, as well as Non-Governmental Organization for solving this serious problem which has created crisis in the country.

(A) Plight of Child Labour Working In Match Industry in Shivakasi

Child labour in Shivakasi is leading a miserable life due to their exploitation by the employers in gross violation of statutory restrictions, in terms of payment of negligible wages, for long working hours and adverse working conditions unsuited to their health and safety. Ms Smithu Kothari a known human rights activist and the editor of Lokyan Bulletin pointed out in her study that the children in the age group of three and a half years (3 1/2 yrs) to fifteen years are made to work for a long span which sometimes extends to twelve hours a day, in degrading and hazardous working conditions. Harbans Singh Committee which submitted its report in the year 1976 highlighted that the majority of child labour in match industry of Shivakasi was employed on piece-rate basis due to the fact that piece-rate wages fixed under the Minimum Wages Act, 1948 provides less wages to the child labour as compared to minimum daily wage payable to them. With the motive of earning more wages the children work much more than their capacity. The nature and extent of exploitation of child labour in match industry of Shivakasi could be easily inferred from the facts brought out by this Committee that inspite of an over twelve hours daily work the young and delicate children between the age group of four to ten years could hardly earn an average of two rupees per day while elder children could earn a maximum amount of rupees six to seven per day.

The plight of child labour in match industry of Shivakasi has not been reduced in any respect even today as is evident from the observations of Smithu Kothari that none of the labour legislation otherwise applicable to child labour are being implemented in most of the units of Shivakasi being unregistered establishments as per Factories Act, 1948. Therefore, the employers do not bother even to maintain a proper record and to provide adequate facilities to the child labour and the employer engages them for period of less than one year with the object to evade statutory liability and for that purpose the inspectors are bribed by the employers so that their drawbacks might be intentionally overlooked by the enforcement machinery which also becomes hand in glove thereby resulting in excessive exploration of the child labour by their employer.

(B) Child Labour in Bidi Making Units

Exploitation of child labour in bidi making units has become a common phenomenon mainly due to the fact that payment is made to the children working in such units on piece rate basis. According to Joseph children of 6 to 12 years are generally, employed in bidi making units. As work is mainly done by infant children of four years accompanying their mothers and they contribute to the out-put of the latter and are socialized in that work environment.

(C) Child Labour in Carpet Industry and Glass Industry

Recently in a study conducted by UNICEF on Child Labour horrifying facts have been brought to the notice of the people that more than one lakh children have been found working in the carpet industry in Mirzapur District of Uttar Pradesh and they were forcibly engaged to do that work and that they did not come to the place of their employment voluntarily rather they were either kidnapped or dragged away by Mafia gangs from their parents to work as child labour in most appalling conditions.

At least 70 per cent of these child weavers working in the woollen hand-knotted carpet industry were beaten and abused while they were in the age group of five to fifteen years. As per UNICEF study the children were not paid only between three to five rupees in lieu of working for fifteen hours and in considerations of three to six thousand knots. These children were found to be suffereing from chronic diseases like anaemia, worms tuberculosis, poor vision and other serious diseases. This study also pointed out that at least fifty thousand children were working for the glass industry in Ferozabad only. These children were exposed to hazardous operations like handling red hard glass, blowing and cutting operations. They were required to sit just six to eight inches away from the hot furnace with temperature varying between 700 C - 1800 C. These children were made to work continuously for twelve hours every day in consideration of meager wage of rupees eight to eleven per day. In Summer season 200-400 glucose drips were given daily to the children as they used to faint due to dehydration and heat exhaustion. According to this study the life span of child workers in Ferozabad is reduced to half and most of the children become victims of tuberculosis and other serious diseases.

(D) Child Labour in Lock-Industry

Another important sector of employment of child labour has been the lock manufacturing industry of Aligarh wherein ten thousand children below the age of fourteen years were found working in the lock-manufacturing industry of Aligarh. They were made to work under unhygienic working conditions adversely effecting their health. Inhalation of paints and thinners on the job damage lungs of the children and some of them have been made to face the danger of loosing their fingers which are caught while they are doing work on machines due to lack of care on the part of the employer as well as on the part of the children due to their immaturity. Sometimes these children loose their lives due to electrocution during electro plating process.

(E) The Pottery Industry of Khurja

Children in thousands are engaged by the employer in the pottery industry of Khurja situated in Uttar Pradesh. Small boys are required to do the work of 'Pick up and putdown' (Uthai Rakhai) of the molds weighing 8 to 12 Kilograms and the children doing such work are commonly called 'phantiwalas'. According to the renowned sociologist Neera Burra who interviewed workers, thekedars (Contractors), master craftsman, children working over-there the boys engaged in the pottery industry are required to pick up empty molds the phanti or a piece o wood on which five to six molds from are usually kept and bring the mold to the potters. Subsequently they carry the filled molds outside and place before the sun to dry then after some-time they carry the half dry pots to the workers for finishing. During the next phase the child labour stack mugs, unload the containers that contain the unbaked clay goods before being fired in the kilns, scrap the power-driven machines used by the potters, remove pebbles from the clay, clean the premises and run errands. The children earn upto 150 rupees a month for an eight-hours day Unskilled workers are paid 200 rupees a month and skilled workers 400 rupees. It has been observed that he workers who worked for fifteen or twenty years earned exactly the same as new adult entrants. It has been observed that the child labour constitutes at least 25 per cent of a total labour force working in pottery industry. A tendency has been observed that he small units employ less than 10 workers so that the Factories' Act, 1948 may not be applicable to such units. Although there is a ban on the employment of the children under the age of 14 years but as smaller units are not covered within the purview of the Factories Act, 1948 so generally they employ children below the age of 14 years.

It ha been observed that neither the workers nor the children are traditional potters and most of them come from the families of agricultural labourers and often, agricultural families send their children to work in the potteries of Khurja.

Children usually supplement family income but in few cases they are even the primary supporters of the family. Most of the children come from Scheduled Caste and muslim families and in few cases adult workers working in such potteries bring their children to do work along with them due to payment of low wages to such adult workers whose income is are engaged by the employer as child labour. It was highlighted by Mrs Burra that he factories owners prefer child labour as compared to adult can not move with that much speed with which children only because the body of the child is lean and thin and they could run fast, bend down and get up quickly without any difficulty. So it could be gathered that the child labour engaged by the owners of the Pottery Industry of Khurja enable the employer to earn maximum profit because meager wages are paid by the employers to such children and there is maximum exploitation of the children over-there without having least regard for the statutory compulsions in vogue against such employers.

(F) Child Labour Working in Tea Gardens of Assam

According to Leela Dubey children are engaged in tea gardens of Assam by the employers not directly as employment below the age of twelve year's children is prohibited under law but due to piece-rate system of wages the children help their parents who are working as full fledged workers in such tea estates. It has been observed that girls under the during the flush season which falls every second month and as each worker is paid according to the weight of the leaves plucked so small girls contribute from one to five Kilograms of such leaves for which payment is claimed by their parents.

As pointed out by various experts on the subject of child labour like Musafir Singh, Kura and Khan, etc., children are generally employed in large numbers in domestic service, tea stalls, and small eating establishments, metal workshops, motor vehicle workshops, cycle repair shops and other shops and commercial establishments. They also seek self-employments as shoe-shiners, hawkers and rag pickers. While doing a all such activities they are subjected to much exploitation and harassment and their contribution to the family income is just nominal in spite of so much harassment.

(G) Children doing Domestic Work

Children are exposed to much harassment while doing house-hold activities such as collection of fuel, fruit and vegetables from the forests, cow-dung, etc. It is quite evident that by doing indispensable house-hold tasks children indirectly contribute substantially to the earning activity of the house-hold by shouldering responsibility of their mother and father so as to enable them to earn more by doing extra work at the place of their employment. In rural areas the children are engaged by their parents in all kinds of agrarian production such as farming, dairy work, as fisherman as well as for the work of craftsman and artisans. In many cottage industries children are engaged by them from generation to generation. It has been rightly observed that by focusing research on the house-hold activities done by the children it could be possible to understand the problem of the child labour in a different understand the problem of the child labour in a different context. It has been quite appropriately observed that after agriculture, cottage industries probably constitute the largest sector employing children and where exploitation of the child labour is a common phenomenon. Many a times in such occupations there would be deception of different types by employing the children as apprentices wherein contractors or middle-man are quite instrumental in the process of exploitation of the child labour in such avocations or employments.

Working Conditions for Child Labour

It has been quite appropriately observed by Mrs Leela Dubey that improvement in the welfare of small children and women should be attempted simultaneously because both these categories of labour often work without wages and their contribution has not generally been formally recognized. Children act as substitutes for mothers at home and both pose a problem for the definitions of 'gainful work' and 'workers'. Moreover, the work of both needs to be viewed in total setting and hence calls for a research for house hold activities in many situations. An understanding of the attitude of elders towards children and their work would also be facilitated by focusing attention on both women and children. In this context it has been further observed by her that it would be advocated to look for deeper causes so as to grasp the nature and magnitude of the children's economic contribution and to understand the economic and cultural cases of this phenomenon. There is an urgent need to evolve research strategies which should ensure that reality might not elude us.

According to Dr. K.D.Gangrade, an expert on child labour the most unhygienic working conditions are those endured by the children who collect rags and other waste materials. Even a causal look at their physique and clothing reveals the extent of their poverty and deprivation as even in the most severe winter, they can be seen working in the open without a single sweater or other protective clothing.

In a recent study conducted by UNICEF it has been brought forth a startling revelation that in the city of Bangalore more than forty thousand street children in the age group of 6 to 16 years are required to pick-up forage and garbage dumps for their survival, Street children move around in places like parks, tourists spots, commercial centres, railway stations and bus-stands barely doing a hard and searching labour through the waste-bins of the city. These children have no permanent place to reside in such big cities and they live on pavements kiosk, under bridges and other places which they find comfortable. The number of the street children has increased enormously in all cities of India, more particularly, in Metropolitan cities and they survive on the basis of collecting paper, plastic waste bottles, rags and other waste material which they subsequently sell for negligible amount in order to earn some money for having their bare necessities. They survive under horrifying conditions and there is an urgent need to improve their lot by providing food and shelter immediately and enable them to get some training so that subsequently they may be in a position to earn adequate amount for their livelihood.

Planning of Programmes to Combat Child Labour

To achieve the object of combating the child labour it is essential to deal with this problem in a well-planned and systematic manner by fixing the priorities for different sectors of employment. For that purpose at the first instance those areas of employment should be taken up where child labour is exposed to excessive exploitation. By adopting that pattern first priority may be given to informal sector of employment because statutory compulsions operating against the employer in the informal sector are just negligible. Sometimes an alternative strategy which may be adopted in the context of the child labour provides for the modes for its abolition in the informal sector, but its feasibility has been be subjected to too much criticism due to the reason that it is bound to increase poverty thereby leading to excessive exploitation of the child labour in some other form or manner. Under these circumstances the only workable strategy would be to support and encourage only few informal activities measures for the protection of the children engaged by them. There could be no doubt that the child labour and its prevalence is not morally justified but it operates in the form of economic compulsion, particularly in t he context of poor masses. So the philosophical approach promoting the idea of child labour necessitate their protection and drive its sanction from the laws forbidding their exploitation.

When we talk of extending protection to any special category of the working class then such approach could have its rational on account of the special position that class or category of workers occupy in the society. Accordingly children and women occupy special position mainly due to the fact that gravity of exploitation to which they are subjected to by their respective employers is more in comparison to the male workers. The idea of child labour has a direct nexus with the poverty as well as lack of education, so immediately an urgency is highlighted for improving the financial condition of parents of such child labour as well as promoting compulsory employment, could take admission in schools for attaining some basic qualifications. It is Common saying that illiteracy is a big curse as it promotes ignorance and by imparting education some wisdom is inculcated in such children who are subsequently in a position to take decision in a wiser manner not feeling bothered about their immediate and urgent problem of supplementing the family income rather having equal botheration in respect of their future prospects and job avenues. The first and foremost requirement is to review the place of the children in the society and to look into the culturally conceived obligation towards them in the context of the human rights as well as expectations of the society from them. The notion that any kind of work that does not constitute either play or education in the strict sense of the terms is always an unjust imposition on the children and that this labour dispossesses them of their childhood, needs to be re-examined. In other words it could be said that it would not at all be justified to presume that only opportunities extended to the children for playing and seeking education are useful for them mainly due to the fact that by playing there is proper growth and development in physical and mental sense in them and education enables them to be the good citizens.

Technical and Vocational Training for Child Labour

It would not be justified to loose of the fact sometime training for some technical job provided to the child would prove to be equally useful to that child in terms of acquiring technical qualifications or the expertise. At the same time it is imperative that the notion of the hard work required to be done by the child labour has to be taken into account in the context of their future prospects. At times this hard work could amount to exploitation in case it operates only in the favour of the employer due to the reason that he gains in terms of profit while children do not at the same time acquire technical experience, in such situation it would be mere exploitation. On the other hand if the hard work rendered by the children operates in the form of apprenticeship or training then it could operate both ways and might be useful both for the employer as well as the concerned children. Under these circumstances an activity may sometimes amount to exploitation of the children but on other occasions it may not amount to exploitation rather could be conveniently termed as apprenticeship or training. Therefore, nature of the work required to be done by the children has to be analyzed in economic and social context. Certain other factors such as payment of remuneration, nature of the work required to be done by the children in the sense of being productive or non-productive work could also help in determining the basic issue, whether such activity would amount to exploitation or not. All these factors should weigh in the mind of the planners as well as the legislation whenever there is proposal to frame basic policies for combating the child labour as well as devising alternative modes for the betterment of the children who instead of being engaged as child labour may be permitted to seek alternatively either schooling in case education is made compulsory or undergo technical training or apprenticeship in order to enable them to have better future in terms of more earning capacity. Role of the legislature is also equally significant due to the fact that the legislature has to enact legislation on the basis of proposals put forth by the planners with the basic object of improving he condition the child labour so as to enable them to be the good citizens and at the same time to earn better wages and consequently enjoy good standard of life in the society.

Programme of Compulsory Education for Children

It is a well known fact that poverty of the parents is a root cause of prevalence of the child labour. Many a times parents in order to avoid starvation take out their children from their schools and get them employed initially either in some domestic employment or in dhabas or tea shops and later on they could be employed in shops and other small scale industries. Most of the children are generally employed in the unorganized sectors employment where they are exposed to maximum exploitation in consideration of meager wages which are paid to them either on weekly or on monthly basis. In this respect it is a common belief that employment of the children is a gainful venture for the poor parents at the sometime employers who are mainly small traders or shop keepers prefer to employ small and delicate children who are sometimes even less than 10 years with a sole object of making maximum profit. Due to these reasons apparently it looks as if both are gainers and nobody looses but in reality small children they are the sufferers as they are deprived of prime opportunity of enjoyable youth period on account doing excessive and strenuous work which adversely affect their normal growth and development. Due to all these factors nation as a whole also ultimately looses because such working children on becoming young neither possess normal health nor requisite stamina for doing good quality work and above all their illiteracy prevents them of the bright future also they are deprived of good carrier and all these factors adversely affect prosperity of the country. One of the basic factors to combat the problem relating to child labour is illiteracy and it is essential that education should be made compulsory in India at least upto the primary level at the first instance. It may not be improper to say that most of the States and the Central Government have on papers declared primary education concerned programmes in the desired spirit due to which in reality illiteracy dominates the scene. Some of the experts claim that the Indian Education system is quite defective because it does offer job-oriented courses for the children in rural and urban areas rather the existing education system prepare the children only of the white collared jobs and such jobs are offered only to few of them and that also after attaining qualification at least upto graduation level due to too much unemployment prevailing in India. So due to these reasons parents as well as children do not take any interest for getting education rather most of them do not bother even to acquaint themselves with the Indian education system by studying in schools even upto primary level, and most of the child labour remain illiterate. Such ignorance operates as a curse thereby seriously hampering the interest of the child labour. There is an urgent need that such ignorance on the part of poor parents should be wiped off from their minds and they should be made to realize that children are not infact source of income for them as is evident from the tendency of having maximum number of children which prevails among them rather a feeling has to be inculcated in their mind that they owe duty responsibility towards their children whom they produce for ensuring that they should acquire proper qualification so that they may be in a position to earn reasonable livelihood so as to ensure in turn the same treatment to their own children. First of all it is imperative for the Government, Central as well as the concerned State Government to provide requisite financial assistance to the poor parents of such children who get such children employed in order to supplement their own meager income. It is the urgent need of the time that the vocational or job oriented studies should be introduced in the Indian education system as an optional course which might be opted by the children of the poor parents and some stipend or subsidy should be paid to the parents of such children who pursue such courses. The basic outlines of such courses should be framed in such a manner that after completing such courses upto middle standard, it might be possible for such children to get absorbed in some suitable jobs specially designed and created for such children so that they may be in a position to have some income and at the same time they may continue to pursue the intensive training programme so that by the time they attain qualification upto the matriculation or higher secondary level they may achieve both the targets, namely, attaining requisite qualifications and obtaining technical training for being absorbed in some suitable profession as a technician or operator or as some other professionally qualified person.

It is a well recognized fact that he ultimate goal of the present education system in vogue has been mainly to make a person a good citizen having requisite etiquettes but it has failed to achieve even these basic goals, mainly due to the fact that officials and the principals of such schools have generally adopted indifferent attitude towards the prevailing education system in India. There is a general feeling prevailing among the common masses that the parents of the child labour have the right to get their children employed and the Governments. In the context of compulsory primary education it has been quite appropriately observed as under :

"The majority of these children (children from tribal, poor and rural families) evade the compulsory laws simply by enrolling in a nearby primary school, with hardly any intention to attend. The teachers usually connive at this stage since it is convenient for them to show large enrollments on paper and actually have a small attendance in class. This enable them to send to the 'higher authorities' good reports on the spread of primary education, while their routine teaching load primary education, while their routine teaching load remains light. Such an arrangement is mutually convenient for everyone concerned i.e. 'children, parents, teachers and even education offices where the 'Coverage' shown by enrollment statistics matters for the preparation of progress reports..."

The aforesaid observation convincingly proves beyond any iota of doubt that compulsory primary education is only a farce and in reality the existing position is just otherwise as majority of the children of poor and down-trodden people from urban and rural areas seek employment at an early age of their childhood instead of attending the school even upto primary level and for this folly the Government, the planners, the officials of education department of the Central and the concerned State Governments, teachers and parents of the child labour all are to be equally blamed for this sorry state of affairs.

The aforesaid view is fully corroborated by the approach adopted by another expert in this field, namely, Dr. Leela Dube who has highlighted the common presumption regarding negative co-relation between child work and formal education due to the fact that an increase in school enrollment and attendance is adversely associated with, or in other words, results in decrease in child employment. So according to her any extension of educational facilities for children would be regarded as an effective remedy against the evil of the child labour and wherever rising school attendance and declining use of child labour would appear together it might be difficult to say which was the effect and which the cause, but the high drop-out rates and low attendance rates would suggest that presence of children might be required elsewhere during school hours. She has quite appropriately observed that it would be erroneous to think that for the rural masses education would be investment towards enhancing earning capacity. It would be advisable that attempt to use education as an instrument for the elimination of the child labour should mainly aim at giving it a more functional outlook and providing it more flexible for whom it was intended. It could suit the requirements of those for whom it was intended. It has been further observed by her in furtherance of this objective as under:

"So long education has only a limited value and so long as children's contributions continue to be essential, perhaps the most practical course would be to restrict the number of hours of work, and organize schools with suitable timings and curricula that would give them the most essential ingredients of education within a short time. If we recognize the indispensability of the child's labour contribution and the desirability of education we have to think about how to combine the two."

It has been convincingly established that compulsory primary education is panacea for the ill of the child labour. So it is high time for the Government to focus attention on the subject of compulsory primary education. It is advisable that a National Commission on the subject of 'Compulsoryu Primary Education and the Child Labour' should be constituted which should extensively undertake the study of brining forth the existing co-relation between the Indian Education system and the child labour and should finally formulate the basic scheme of compulsory primary education particularly in the context of the child labour wherein the aspect of vocational guidance and training should be given top-priority at least under the optional system of legal education which may be exclusively meant for the poor masses whose children generally get employed at an early age. For such people employment-oriented educational scheme for primary and middle level should be evolved in a detailed manner as discussed above which may not only ensure imparting of education to the poor children rather it should also guarantee employment to them after getting school education. In furtherance of this objective the government of India has re-structured for scholarships has been increased and special awards introduced to encourage schooling of children, particularly of workers in 36A unorganized sector, so as to provide requisite incentive to them and at the same time enable them to get some monetary assistance which they could be in a position to receive by to overcome their starvation conditions and supplement their meager income by financial assistance provided to them in lieu of continuance of their children in schools under compulsory education system.

Task Force Committee on the Child Labour under the Chairmanship of Dr. L.M.Singhvi felt that a more meaningful and effective educational policy was called for which should ensure change of curriculum and promote integration of educational requirements with local crafts which should also ensure greater involvement of voluntary agencies and changes and adjustments in the schedule of vacations and holidays to coincide with environments.

From the aforesaid recommendations of Task Force Committee it could be easily gathered that a meaningful and effective educational policy could result in prevention of exploitation of the children of the tender age by the employers and it would be imperative that educational requirements should be integrated with crafts and other vocational courses in order to ensure that the educational programme should become employment oriented as discussed above. It would not be unjustified to expect that involvement of voluntary agencies as well as non-governmental organizations (NGOs) would certainly be more meaningful in order to implement the compulsory education programme for the children in the right perspective due to the fact that such agencies are well acquainted with the problem of the child labour, so their acquaintance with the basic problem would prove to be quite useful in formulating and enforcing compulsory educational policy for the children including the child labour below the age of prescribed compulsory schooling.

The Task Force Committee had also underlined and recommended comprehensive statutory provisions for providing educational facilities for child workers and as per their recommendation education should be made as a part of the labour welfare measures to be adopted by the employers. It also recommended arrangements for non-formal education in areas where there was concentration of working children. The government felt that it was not feasible to make any statutory provision in labour laws for providing education facilities to child workers but it was otherwise of the view that the employers should be encouraged to import education to such workers as a part of labour welfare measures. So far as the recommendation regarding non-formal education was concerned the government has long back accepted the recommendation and assured that suitable arrangements would be made for non-formal education in areas where there was concentration of working children. It is quite certain that non-formal education would increase literacy among child labour and hence would prove to be quite useful and serve meaningful purpose.

There is no doubt that the condition of the child workers would improved a lot in case welfare measures including educational facilities and vocational guidance as appear recommendations of the experts and the Task Force Committee are enforced to improve the competence and capabilities of the child labour. The experience gained so far with regard to the child labour has established that measures in the form of statutory and non-statutory steps to combat the child labour could not prove to be so much effective unless social awakening is created among the common masses and public opinion is built up against the employers exploiting the child labour general public who could in turn persuade the employer that they should not exploit the child labour and such social action could ultimately have reformative impact on the employers who grievances of the child labour and such changed attitude of the employer would ultimately lead to admissibility of improved working and living conditions to the child labour.

Recent Measures Undertaken by State to Combat the Child Labour

An effective scheme to combat the child labour has been enforced by the Ministry of Labour, Government of India in collaboration with UNICEF and in furtherance of this Programme a Child Labour Institute since September, 1990, at the first instance for a period of three years with the financial assistance provided by the UNICEF, with the main objective of drafting documents and conducting research studies pertaining to the conditions of child labour in various industries situated in different regions of India For the purpose of creating public awakening and for the purpose of providing requisite training to various officials concerned with the working children, various films and distribution of printed material are adopted for projecting the existing condition of child labour.

It is high time for the Government to realize that problem pertaining to child labour is quite complex one and it may not be possible for the Government to achieve success unless it seeks active cooperation from other concerned quarters by ensuring active involvement of experts, activists, planners, administrators and above all non-governmental organizations already working in the area of the child labour. Although said lines but it is desirable on its part to associate all these people consistently from its inception to the conclusion of the Action Programme and there should be total involvement of all such persons at each and every stage of the work. In this context it has been rightly planned by the Ministry of Labour that training may be imparted to officials and NGOs working in area of child labour. At the some time there is urgent need training programmes and conducting research activities on short term as well as long term basis by offering fellowships as well as through action research projects. In this regard it is also made known that child Labour Cell has already taken up task of publishing reports and studies on street children in selected cities, prepared summaries of child labour in various industries, published select bibliography on child labour and taken up work of documentation on child labour. After evaluating approach of the Ministry of Labour in the context of the child labour undertaken in cooperation with the UNICEF, it may reasonably be hoped that positive and meaningful purpose will be served by all these programmes and it may probably improve the lot of child labour in the coming decade or in other words by the end of this century and the new century may start with a hope of better future for the child labour in terms of improved working and living conditions for them..

11

Child Labour In India

According to a recent ILO estimate, there are 52 million working children in the world. Of these, approximately 29 million are from South Asia, 10 million from Africa, 9 million from East Asia and 3 million from Latin America and only one million will originate from developed countries.

Out of the 29 million working children in South Asia, 10.7 million child workers are estimated to be in India (1971 census). Out of total population of 548 million recorded in 1971 census, about 230 million were children below 15 years, i.e., 42 % of the total population. The number of child workers according to the 1971 census was 10.7 million as against 14.5 million recorded in 1961 census. This step decline can be assigned to the conceptual differences in the definition of 'workers' adopted in the 1971 census. Proceeding logically on the basis of the increase in population and the trends in the economy, the actual volume of child labour is likely to be much higher than the estimated 10.7 million from 1971 census. Children constitute 5.9 per cent of the total labour force of the economy.

The percentage of child labour to total population is as high as 9.24 in Andhra Pradesh whereas it is as low as 1.30 per cent in Kerala. Of the bulk of child labour in country, nearly 93 per cent are in rural areas and rest in urban areas. According to ILO estimate, 80 per cent of these working children would be classified as 'unpaid family workers.' The great majority of these children are in agriculture or in small scale industries in rural area and in workshops, petty shops and quasi-family undertakings in urban areas. Seventy-nine per cent of the child workers are said to be employed as cultivators, agricultural labourers, all over the country. Eight per cent are engaged in livestock, forestry, plantation, etc., about 6 per cent manufacturing and processing and another 6 per cent in household and other services industries and the rest in trade, commerce and transport.

The first all India Agricultural Labour Enquiry conducted by the Ministry of Labour revealed that 4.9 per cent of the total agricultural labour force were children in 1950-51. It was 7.7 per cent in 1956-57, 7.4 million children are engaged in agriculture according to the 1971 census. The Rural Labour Enquiry conducted by the Ministry of Labour revealed that child agriculture labourers constitute 6 pre cent of the total agricultural labour force in 1964-65.

Like most problems in India, child labour emerges out of the socio-economic conditions prevailing in the economy. Children are often forced to work due to economic needs and social conditions. Whatever might be the conditions leading to the children seeking employment-for economic considerations or otherwise, it conditions detrimental to their health, welfare and development. Most of these children have never been to school or have dropped out of schools at some stage or the other. A working child is deprived of education, training and acquiring skills which are pre-requisites for earning, sustaining and for economic development. The perception of child labour as a social problem has become an public, trade unions, welfare and social service organizations and the state.

CONSTITUTIONAL PROVISIONS

Article 24 of the Indian Constitution lays down:

"No child below the age of 14 years shall be employed to work in any factory or mine or engaged in any other hazardous employment."

Article 39(c) lays down that 'the health, strength of workers-man, woman and the tender age of children are not abused and that citizens are not forced by economic necessity to enter avocation unsuited to their age or strength.

Article 39(c) proclaims:

"The childhood and youth are protected against exploitation and against moral and material abandonment."

OTHER LEGISLATIONS

With a view to eradicate the problems of child labour the following legislations have been enacted regulating the employment of children:

The Children (Pledging of Labour) Act, 1933. The Act defines 'child' as person who is under the age of 15 years. The Act prohibits the making of agreements to pledge the labour of children and the employment of children whose labour has been pledged. The Act also lays down that any agreements or contracts to pledge the labour of a child is void and imposes penalties on any such agreement or employment of a pledged child.

The second Act relates to the Employment of Children

Act, 1938.

Section 3(1): No child who has not completed his fifteenth year shall be employed or permitted to work in any occupation-

(a) connected with transport of passengers, goods or mails by railway, or

(b) Connected with a port authority within the limits of any port, or

(c) Connected with cinder picking, clearing of an ash pit or building operation, in the railway premises, or

(d) Connected with the work in a watering establishment, at a railway station, involving the management of a vendor or any other employee of the establishment from one platform to another or into or out of a moving train, or

(e) Connected with the work relating to the construction of railway station or with any other where such work is done in close proximity to or between the railway lines.

Section 3(3): No child who has not completed his fourteenth year shall be employed or permitted to work in any workshop where any of the process set in the schedule is carried on.

The Schedule

(1) bidi-making; (2) carpet weaving; (3) cement manufacturing, including bagging of cement; (4) cloth printing, dying and weaving; (5) manufacturing of matches, explosives and fire-works; (6) mica-cutting and splitting; (7) shellac manufacture; (8) soap manufacture; (9) tanning; and (10) wool cleaning.

Several other legislations and Acts have laid down special provisions and clauses pertaining to the employment of children.

I. The 'child is defined as follows in the different Acts:

1.Beedi & Cigar workers (Conditions of Employment) Act, 1966,

Sec. 2(b): 'Child' means a person who has not completed 14 years of age.

2. Factories Act, 1948 and Minimum Wages Act, 1948, Sec. 2(c): 'Child' means a person who has not completed his fifteenth year of age.

3. Mines Act, 1952, Sec. 2(c): 'Child' means a person who has not completed his fifteenth year.

4. Motor Transport Workers Act, 1961, Sec. 2(c): 'Child' means a person who has not completed his fifteenth year.

5. Plantations Labour Act, 1951, Sec 2(c): 'Child' means a person who has not completed his fifteenth year.

II. The minimum age of employment of a child is given in various Acts as follows:

1. Factories Act, 1948, Sec. 67: No child who has not completed his fourteenth year shall be required to or allowed to work in any factory.

2. Mines Act, 1952, Sec. 45: No child shall be employed in any mines nor shall any child be allowed to be present in any part of mine which is below ground or in any (open cast working) in which any mining operation is carried on.

3. Plantation Labour Act, 1951, Sec. 24: No child who has not completed his twelfth year shall be required or allowed to work in any plantation.

4. Indian Merchant Shipping Act, 1958, Sec. 109: No person under fifteen years of age shall be engaged or carried to sea to work in any capacity in any ship, except

(a) in a school ship or training ship, in accordance with the prescribed conditions; or

(b) in a ship in which all persons employed two hundred tones gross; or

(c) in a home-made ship of less than two hundred tons gross; or

(d) where such person is to be employed on nominal wages and will be in the charge of his father or other adult near male relative.

5. Motor Transport Workers Act, 1961, Sec. 21: No child who has not completed to work in any capacity,

6. Beedi and Cigar Workers (Conditions of Employment) Act, 1966, Sec. 24: No child who has not completed his fourteenth year shall be required or allowed to work in any industrial premises.

7. State Shops and Commercial Establishment Acts

The minimum age of employment in shops and commercial establishments is 12 years in Bihar, Gujarat, J&K, Madhya Pradesh, Karnataka, Orissa, Rajasthan, Tripura, Uttar Pradesh, West Bengal, Goa, Daman and Diu and Manipur, and 14 years in Andhra Pradesh, Assam, Haryana, Himanchal Pradesh, Kerala, Tamil Nadu, Punjab, Delhi, Chandigarh, Pondicherry and Meghalaya. The Minimum age of employment is 15 years in Maharashtra. There are no separate shops and commercial establishments Acts in Andaman & Nicobar, Arunachal Pradesh, Dadra & Nagar Haveli, Lakshdweep, Nagaland & Sikkim.

8. **Radiation Protection Rules,** 1971, Persons below 18 years cannot be employed under the Radiation protection Rules, 1971

9. Apprentices Act, 1961, Sec. 3(a): A person shall not be qualified for being engaged as an apprentice to undergo apprenticeship training in any designated trade, unless he is not less than 14 years of age.

10. The Children (Pledging of Labour) Act, 1933, Sec. 3: An agreement to pledge the labour of a child (below 15) shall be void.

III. Prohibition of allowing children to work in hazardous occupations under the Factories Act, 1948 is given below:

1. Factories Act, 1948, Sec. 22(2): No young person shall be allowed to clean, lubricate or adjust any part of prime mover or of any transmission machinery while the prime mover or transmission machinery is in motion, or to clean, lubricate or adjust any part of machine if the cleaning, lubrication or adjustment thereof would expose the young person to risk of injury from any moving part either of that machine or of any adjacent machinery.

Section 23(1): No young person shall work at any machine to which this section applies unless he has been fully instructed as to the dangers arising in connection with the machine and the precautions to be observed and-(a) he received sufficient training in work at machine, or (b) is under adequate supervision by a person who has a thorough knowledge and experience of the machine.

Section 23(2): Sub-section (1) shall apply to such machines as may be prescribed by the (State) Government, being machines which in its opinion are of such a dangerous character that young person ought not to work at them unless the foregoing requirements are complied with.

Section 27: No child shall be employed in any part of a factory for pressing cotton in which a cotton-opener is at work:

Provided that if the feed-end of a cotton opener is in a room separated from the delivery end by a partition extending to the roof or to such height as the inspector may in any particular case specify in writing; children may be employed on the side of the partition where the feed-end is situated.

Section 34(2): The (State) Government may make rules prescribing the maximum weights which may be lifted, carried or moved by children employed in factories or any class or description of factories or in carrying on any specified process.

IV. The hours of work for children are regulated as

follows:

1. Factories Act, 1948, Sec. 7(a): No child shall be employed or permitted to work in any factory for more than 4 and 1/2 hours a day.

2. Minimum wages (Central) Rules, 1950, Sec. 24: The number of hours which shall constitute a normal working day shall be 4 and 1/2 hours in case of a child.

3. Plantation Labour Act, 1951, Sec. 19: No child shall be required or allowed to work on any plantation for more than 40 hours a week.

4. State Shops and Commercial Establishment Acts The hours of work for young persons in shops and commercial establishment are 7 per day in Andhra Pradesh, Bihar, Tamil Nadu, Tripura, Pondicherry and West Bengal: 6 per day in Gujarat, Maharashtra, Jammu & Kashmir, Uttar Pradesh and Delhi: 5 per day in Himanchal Pradesh, Madhya Pradesh, Karnataka, Orissa an Punjab and 3 per day in Rajasthan.

5. Apprentices Rules, 1962, Sec. 8: The weekly hours of work of an apprentice while undergoing practical training shall be as follows:

(i) The total number of hours per week shall be 42 to 48 hours (including the time spent on related instructions);

(ii) Apprentices undergoing basic training shall ordinarily work for 42 hours per week including the time on the related instructions;

(iii) Apprentices during the second year of apprenticeship shall work for 42 to 45 hours per week including the time spent on related instructions;

(iv) Apprentices during the third and subsequent years of apprenticeship shall work for the same number of hours per week as the workers in trade in the establishments in which the apprentices is undergoing apprenticeship training: Provided however, that short-term apprentices may be engaged to work up to a limit hours per week.

V. Children are prohibited from working at night according to the following Acts:

1.Factories Act, 1948, Sec. 71(b): No child shall be employed or permitted to work in any factory during night.

(For the purpose of this Section 'night' shall mean a period of at least twelve consecutive hours which shall include the interval between 10 p.m. to 6 a.m.)

2. Plantation Labour Act, 1951, Sec. 25: Except with the permission of the State Government, no child worker shall be employed in any plantation otherwise than between the hours of 6 am and 7 pm.

3. Beedi and Cigar Workers (Conditions of Employment) Act, 1966, Sec. 25: No young person shall be required or allowed to work in any industrial premises except between 6 a.m. and 7 p.m.

(Young person means a person who has completed 14 years of age but has not attained 18 years of age.)

4.State Shops and Commercial Establishments Acts, Night work for children and young person also prohibited under State laws relating to shops and commercial establishments. The children and young persons are allowed to work between 6 a.m. and 7 p.m. in Andhra Pradesh, Gujarat, Maharashtra, Tamil Nadu, Pondicherry; 7a.m. to 7 p.m. in Bihar and Kerala; 7 a.m. to 9 p.m. in Jammu & Kashmir and Madhya Pradesh; 6 a.m. to 8 p.m. in Karnataka; 6 a.m. to 10 p.m. in Orissa and Rajasthan and 8 a.m. to 8 p.m. during Winter and 7 a.m. to 9 p.m. during summer in Delhi. They cannot be employed after 8 p.m. in West Bengal and Tripura.

5. Apprentices Rules, 1962, Sec. 8(2): No apprentice, other than a short term apprentice, shall be engaged in such training between the hours of 10 p.m. and 6 a.m. except with the prior approval of the Apprenticeship Adviser who also shall

give his approval if he is satisfied that it is in the interest of the training of the apprentice or the public interest.

INTERNATIONAL ORGANIZATIONS

The United Nations declaration of the rights of the child on November 20, 1959 lays down that the child shall enjoy special protection and shall be given opportunities and facilities by law and by other means to enable them to socially in a healthy and normal manner and in conditions of freedom and dignity. In the enactment of laws for this paramount consideration.

The Children's charter stipulates that for every child a community which recognizes and plans for his needs protects him against physical dangers, moral hazards and diseases, provides him with safe and wholesome places for play and recreation and makes provision for his cultural and social needs.

PROVISIONS IN ILO

In the interest of the working children all over the world, the International Labour Organization has adopted 18 conventions as follows:

1. Minimum Age (Industry) Convention (No. 5), 1919.
2. Minimum Age (Sea) Convention (No. 7), 1920.
3. Minimum Age (Agriculture) Conventions (No. 10), 1921.
4. Minimum Age (Trimmer and Stokers) Convention (No. 15), 1921.
5. Minimum Age (Non-Industrial Employment) Convention (No. 33), 1932.
6. Minimum Age (Sea) Convention (Revised) (No. 58), 1936.
7. Minimum Age (Industry) Convention (Revised) (No. 59), 1937.
8. Minimum Age (Non-Industrial Employment) Convention

(Revised) (No. 60), 1937.

9. Minimum Age (Underground Work) Convention (No. 123), 1973.

10. Minimum Age Convention (No. 138),1973.

11. Medical Examination of Young Persons (Sea) Convention (No. 16), 1921.

12. Medical Examination (Sea fearers) Convention (No. 73), 1946.

13. Medical Examination of Young Persons (Industry) Convention (No. 77), 1946.

14. Medical Examination of Young Persons (Non-Industrial Occupation) Convention (No. 78), 1946.

15. Medical Examination of Young Persons (Underground Work) Convention (No. 124), 1965.

16. Night Work of Young Persons (Industry) Convention (No. 6), 1919.

17. Night Work of Young Persons (Non-Industrial Occupations) Convention (No. 79), 1946.

18. Night Work of Young Persons (Industry) Convention (Revised) (No. 90), 1948.

The Government of India have ratified 6 of the 18 conventions adopted by the ILO for children and young person. Following are the 6 conventions which have been ratified and implemented in the country:

1. Minimum Age (Industry) Convention (No. 5), 1919.

2. Minimum Age (Trimmer and Stokers) Convention (No. 15), 1921.

3. Minimum Age (Underground Work) Convention (No. 123), 1973.

4. Medical Examination of Young Persons (Sea) Conven-

tion (No. 16), 1921.

5. Night Work of Young Persons (Industry) Convention (No.6), 1919.

6. Night Work of Young Persons (Industry) Convention (Revised No. 9), 1948.

One of the most important conventions is the Minimum Age Convention, 1973 which prescribed the minimum age as not less than 15 years for developed countries and 14 years for initial fixation by developing countries. For hazardous occupations, the minimum age fixed is 18. Fixing of minimum age for admission to employment needs to be preceded by creation of a suitable enforcement machinery. To set up such a machinery, particularly for the unorganized sectors in agriculture, cottage and heavy industries, small scale industries, etc. becomes a difficult task in a developing country.

A Resolution was adopted in the International Labour Conference in its 65th Session in 1979 in the International Year of Child for the protection elimination of Child Labour and for the Transitional measures to be adopted by the countries (Please see page 182).

Notwithstanding the constitutional provisions, Acts and legislations and documentary disapprovals, child labour is an empirical reality present in differential degree in almost all the sectors of our national economy, organized or unorganized, regulated or unregulated.

The National Commission on Labour has observed in its report that the employment of children is more of an economic problem than anything else. The Commission felt that the denial of opportunity to children for their proper physical development and for education is a serious issue keeping in view the larger interest of the society. The Commission has recommended that it is necessary to give the child education in his formative years and this can be ensured by fixing the employment hours of children so as to enable them to attend school. The Commission has also recommended that where the number of children is adequate, the employers, with the assistance of the State Governments, should make arrangements to combine work education.

The VIth Plan aims at universal primary education, increase in employment opportunities and improvement in family incomes. It is hoped that children will thus gradually be beaned away from work and sent to school.

COMMITTEE ON CHILD LABOUR

With a view to studying the problems of child labour and to suggest suitable measures for their protection and welfare, the Ministry of Labour, Government of India, has set up a Committee, in its Resolution dated 6/7th February, 1979. The following are the terms of reference of the Committee:

(i) Examine existing laws, their adequacy and implementation, and suggest corrective action to be taken to improve implementation and to remedy defects.

(ii) Examine the dimensions of child labour, the occupations in which children are employed, etc., and suggest new areas where laws abolishing/regulating the employment of children can be introduced.

(iii) Suggest welfare measures, training and other facilities which would be introduced to benefit children in employment.

The Committee has been up a plan of action for making an in-depth and diagnostic study on the nature and extent of the problem adequacy of existing legal framework and the supportive measures. The Committee will be taking up case studies in different blocks in about eight selected states to study the rural conditions and right also be doing sectoral studies in the organized and unorganized sectors where the incidence of child labour is quite high. The Committee has also brought out a questionnaire to elicit information on child labour from the public, the politician, trade unions, social welfare and other institutions, employers, parents of children and Government organizations. The information received from the questionnaire will be tabulated and utilized in the report of the Committee.

The Committee on Child Labour is expected to make recommendations, inter alia, on the following main issues:

(i) prescribing a uniform minimum age for employment of children under all the Acts.

(ii) identify hazardous occupations and banning the employment of children in such occupations.

(iii) recommending laws, rules, regulations, Acts and legislations for protecting children in employment and for progressive elimination of child labour. and

(iv) suggesting labour welfare and social welfare measures to protect the working children from exploitation and suitable machinery for enforcement and implementation of provisions adopted for welfare of working children.

A child labour cell has set p to formulate, coordinate and to implement policies and programmes for the welfare of child labour. At present, the cell is assisting the committee on Child Labour. It is expected to take follow up action on the recommendations of the Committee on Child Labour.

RESOLUTION

Concerning the International Year of the Child and the Progressive Elimination of Child Labour & Transitional Measures adopted by the International Labour Conference in its sixty-fifth Session (1979) at Geneva.

The General Conference of the International Labour Organization.

Recalling resolution 31/169 adopted by the United Nations General Assembly, proclaiming 1979 as the International Year of the Child with general objectives of promoting the well-being of children, drawing attention to their special needs and encouraging national action on behalf of children, particularly for the least privileged and those who are at work.

Noting the activities that were undertaken at the national, regional and international levels in preparation for the International Year of the Child and the progress made since.

Convinced that the International Year of the Child provides for all member States an opportunity to review their economic and social policies concerning child welfare and to formulate guidelines in this sphere.

Considering that a new and fair international economic order would greatly contribute towards genuine economic and social development, primarily of benefit to children.

Recalling the endorsement by the ILO of the aims of the International Year of the Child and its pledge to make every effort and lend all support to member States for their earliest possible fulfillment.

Recalling the United Declaration of the Right of the Child, 1959, and particularly Principle 9, which stipulates that the child should be protected against all forms of neglect, cruelty and exploitation; that he should not be admitted to employment before an appropriate minimum age; and that he should in no case be caused or permitted to engage in any occupation or employment which would prejudice his health or education, or interfere with his physical, mental or moral development.

Considering that since its foundation the International Labour Organization has sought to eliminate child labour and to provide protection for children.

Noting with approval the Director-General's Declaration on the International Year of the Child.

Deeply concerned that child labour still remains widespread

in many parts of the world and that working children frequently work under conditions including those of exploitation detrimental to their age or strength.

Recognizing the need to ensure that the health and strength and the tender age of children are not abused and that children are not permitted to enter avocations unsuited to their age or strength.

Considering that the International Year of the Child should be an occasion to reaffirm with practical measures and deeds that the well-being of today's children is the concern of all people everywhere.

Recalling the decision of the Governing Body of the International Labour Office, taken at its 208th Session (November 1978) to request the Member States to supply a report in 1980 under Article 19 of the Constitution on the extent to which effect has been given or is proposed to be given to the Minimum Age Convention (No. 138) and Recommendation (No. 146) of 1973.

1. Calls upon member States to strengthen effort for the elimination of child labour and for the protection of children, and in this context :

(a) to implement the provision of the Minimum Age Convention, 1973 (No. 138) and, where they not already done so, to ratify this Convention as early as practicable;

(b) to ensure in particular full recognition of the principle that any work undertaken by children who have not completed their compulsory education shall not be such as would prejudice their education or development;

(c) to apply the Minimum Age Recommendation, 1973 (No.146), and the Minimum Age (Underground Work) Recommendation, 1965 (No. 124);

(d) to report in detail in 1980 under the procedure of Article 19 of the Constitution on the progress reached in the implementation of the Minimum Age Convention (No. 138) and Recommendation (No. 146), 1973.

(e) pending the elimination of child labour, to take all necessary social and legislative action for the progressive elimination of child labour and, during the transitional period until the elimination of child labour to regulate and humanize it and to give particular attention to the implementation of special standards of children relating to medical examination, night work, underground work, working hours, weekly rest, paid annual leave and certain types of hazardous and dangerous work embodied in a number of ILO instruments.

(f) to make every effort to extend the provisions of appropriate educational facilities, in order fully to apply compulsory education and to introduce it where it does not exist and, where education is compulsory, to make it effective;

(g) to ensure that appropriate protective labour legislation applies to all children at work in the sectors of activity in which they are employed;

(h) to ensure that special attention is given to the provision of fair remuneration and to its protection for the benefit of the child;

(i) to strengthen, where appropriate, labour inspection and to undertake all other measures conductive to the elimination of child labour;

(j) (i) to identify the special needs of children to strengthen efforts to improve the general economy and social well-being of the family, and to launch a national campaign aimed at creating awareness among the general public of the adverse effects of child labour on his/ her development;

(ii) to develop international solidarity and cooperation with the developing countries and to activate efforts to establish a new and fair international economic order so as to respond more effectively to the basic measures undertaken by each State for better child protection.

2. Calls upon government and employer's and worker's organizations to assess the situation of child work and to assist the competent bodies and the ILO to strengthen their action programme for children.

3. Invites the Governing Body of the International Labour Office to instruct the Director-General to continue and reinforce the ILO's action through such means as factual survey of national situations and practices for the elimination of child labour and for the protection of children at work, and to make the necessary preparations for a global revision of the relevant ILO instruments.

References

IPEC Programme Document, (International Labour Organization, Geneva. 1992-93).

Conditions of Work Digest-Child Labour Law and Practice, Vol. X, 27 (1991).

Towards the abolition of child labour: ILO Policy and its implications for ILO technical cooperation activities, 6 (ILO Publication, 1993).

IPEC Programme Document, 1 (International Labour Office, Geneva 1992-93).

IPEC Programme Document, 7 (International Labour Office, 1992-93).

Article 1 to Article 3 of the Convention No. 138 of the International Labour Conference-Minimum Age Convention, 1973.

Children and Work in India 1992-A Reference Annual, 65 (Publication-Division, Government of India).

The Hindustan Times, Wednesday, February 6, 1991, 3 (New-Delhi Edn.).

"The Economic Role of Children in India: Methodological Issues', 179 to 213 at 182, 'Child Work Poverty and Under development', Edited by Garry Rogers and Guy Standing (ILO, Geneva, 1981).

Children at Work, Edited by Elias Menedelievich at 81 (ILO, Geneva, 1979).

Upendra Baxi, "The Crisis of the Indian Legal System', 5, New Delhi Vikas Publications, 1982.

Fernandes Walter, 'Child Labour and the Process of Exploitation', "The Indian Journal of Social Work, Volume No. III, No. 2, 171-190 at 174 (April, 1992).

"Urban Informal Sector: A profile of Marginalised Irregulars" Social Action Vol. 40 (2) April- June, 126-145.

Fernandes Walter, 'Child Labour and the Process of Exploitation, "The Indian Journal of Social Work, Volume L.III, No.2, 191-190 at 174, April, 1992.

Neera Burra, 'Health Hazards Seminal 350, October 1988, Child Labour Special Issue at 25.

The Hindustan Times, Wednesday, June 16, 1993. 11 New Delhi

The Economic Times, June 16 1993 at 2 New Delhi

The Hindustan Times, June 16, 1993 at 11 New Delhi

The Economic Times, Jan. 20, 1993, 4 New Delhi

The Hindustan Times, October 6, 1992, 3 New Delhi

The Times of India, March 8, 1993, 10 New Delhi

Estimates supplied by Independent Agencies.

National Sample Survey.

The Times of India, March 8, 1993, 10 (New Delhi Edn.)

Constitution (42nd Amendment) Act, 1976.

A.I.R. 1991 S.C.417.

A.I.R. 1982 SC 1473.

Jayaram C., 'Salient Features of Child Labour Act, 1986,' 1989 Lab I.C. 50 (Journal Section) at 51.

The Hindu, April 24, 1986, 8 (Hyderabad Edn.)

A.I.R. 1991 SC 417.

'Government Adopts New Child Labour Policy' The Hindu, August 13, 1987 1, (Hyderabad Edn.)

ILO 'Child Labour at Work', 6 (1979).

Ex-Director, Indian Law Institute, New Delhi.

Dr. S.N.Fain, 'Child Labour 23 J.I.L.I. 336, (1981).

For details see, 'Dr. G. Varandani 'Minimum Age of Employment and Medical Examination of Children and Adolescent, Kurukshetra Law Journal, Vol. 7 (1981) 101 to 118.

Gengrade, K.D. 'Dimensions of Social Work in India' pp. 45-46 (1976 edn. Marwah Publications)

The Hindustan Times, November 15, 1992, 3 (New Delhi Edn.)

Kothari, Smithu 'There's Blood on those Match sticks', Law & Poverty - Critical Essays', 322 (Tripathi Publications, 1988-edn.)

'Child Workers in the Informal Sector of N.G.Os- Some reflections', 'Women and Child Workers in unorganized Sector', 75 (1988 edn.).

The Hindustan Times. Oct., 6 1992, 3 (New Delhi End.)

Burra, Neera, A Report on Child Labour in the Pottery Industry (New Delhi, DANDIA, November 1987).

"Child Work, Poverty and Under Development" edited by Grey Rodgers and Guy Standing (I.L.O., Geneva, 1981.)

"Child Work, Poverty and Under Development" edited by Grey Rodgers and Gay Standing at 209, (ILO Geneva, 1981.).

"Children at Work," Edited by Elias Mendelievich at 84 (ILO, Geneva, 1987).

The Hindustan Times, June 13, 1993, 9 (New Delhi Edn.)

"Child Work, Poverty and under Development" Edited by Grey Rogers and Guy Standing, at 179, (ILO, Geneva, 1981).

'Chitra Naik"An Action-Research Project on Universal Primary Education, Indian Institute Education Bulletin, 2 (1981) at 137.

"Child Work, Poverty and Under-Development Edited by Grey Rodgers and Guy Standing, 179-213 at 205.

The Hindustan Times, September 29, 1993, 24 (New Delhi Edn.)

Source: India 1992 - a reverencer Annual, Publication Division,

Government of India at 627.

Rao, T.V., Verma, K.K., Khandelwal, A.K., E.Abraham, S.J. (1989): Alternation Approaches and Strategies of Human Resource Development, Rawat Publications, Jaipur.

Mehta, M.M. (1976): Human Resources Development Planning: with special reference to Asia and the Far East. The Macmillan company of India Ltd., New Delhi.

Munjal, Satish (1989), Human Resources and Rural Development Printwell Publishers, Jaipur.

Seventh Fiver Year Plan 1985-90, Mid-Term Appraisal

Government of India, Planning commission.

There has been a slight reduction of 3 per cent in work-force in agriculture between 1971 and 1981.

Statement made by the Minister of State for Planning in reply to a question in Parliament on August 1, 1985.

Agarwal, B.L. (1983), 'Changing Pattern of Employment and Income in India, paper presented by Prof. Gautam Mathur to ADIPA conference, Kualalumpur.

Mathur, Gautam (1983), 'Employment and Inter-generational Equity', presented to International Economic Association conference, Poona, 1980, published in Austin Robinson, P.R.Brahmanand and L.K. Deshpandu, etc.,Employment Policy in a developing Country, vol,1, Macmillan Press Ltd. London, 1983, pp. 253-271.

Agarwal, B.L. and Ramamurthy, T.V. (1984). Formation of Elements of Employment strategy consistent with the overall Plan objections and consideration for Feasibility of Time Bound Plan for Fuller Employment of 2000 A.D., IAMR, (Draft)and Gautam Mathur and T.V. Ramamurthy, perspections of Industrialisation in the VII Plan, in Seventh Plan Perspectives, ed. Dr.Malcolm Adisheshiah, 1985.

Mathur Gautam, (1976). Higher Education and Employment in Sudan A Book Review.

Harbison, F. and Myers, C.A.,(1964) Education, Manpower and Economic Growth: Strategies to Human Resource Development.

Gautam Mathur, Memorandum to the Education Commission as member of Task Force on Educational Planning.

Panchmukhi P.R.,(1975), Devaluation of Education A Quantitative Analysis, Journal of Higher Education, Vol.1

Mathur Gautam,(1935). The Skill-Placement Correspondence in Higher Education in Eighties, (Ed.)J.Veeraraghavan, C.D. Deshmukh Commemoration Volume, Delhi.

Mathur Gautam,(1978). Active Education for Manpower Development.

Agarwal B.L. and Soni N.K., Industry Occupation Matrix, vol.I, IAMR (Draft).

The success ratio of graduates had dropped down from 1/27 in 1971 to 1/64 in 1978, and that of post-graduates from 1/8 in 1971 to 1/17 in 1978, and so on. See B.L. Agarwal, Nexus Between Jobs and Education, in Higher Education in Eighties, C.D.Deshmukh Commemoration Volume, ed.J.Veera Raghvan, Delhi, 1985.

Abbreviations

RBD	Registration of Births and Deaths Act, 1969
MCH	Maternal and Child Health
NNT	neo-natal tetanus
FNB	Food and Nutrition Board
IMR	infant mortality rate
CD	Community Development
IRDP	Integrated Rural Development Programme
CSWB	Central Social Welfare Board
ICDS	Child Development Service Schemes
DWCRA	Development of Women and Children in Rural Areas
EPI	Expanded Programme of Immunization
ANP	Applied Nutrition Programme
IDP	Intensive Development Programme
SNP	Special Nutrition Programme
BNP	Balwadi Nutrition Programme
MDM	Mid-day Meal Programme
PANA	Prophylaxis Against Nutritional Anaemia
DWCRA	Development of Women and Children in Rural Areas
PEO	Programme Evaluation Organization
GDP	Gross Domestic Product
NFE	non-formal education
NIOH	National Institute of Occupational Health
CLTAC	Child Labour Technical Advisory Committee
IPEC	International Programme for Elimination of Child Labour
IGEP	Indo-German Economic Project
TISS	Tate Institute of Social Sciences
NREP	National Rural Employment Programme
RLEGP	Rural Landless Employment Guarantee Programme
NCERT	National Council of Educational Research and Training
RFLP	Rural Functional Literacy Project
SAEP	State Adult Education Programme
VA	Voluntary Agencies

JETS	Joint Evaluation Teams
NAAE	National Authority for Adult Education
COSIP	College Science Improvement Programmes
COHSSIP	College Humanities and Social Improvement Programmes
MIMI	mechanized light machinery
OLS	Operation Lifeline Sudan
UNRRA	United Nations Relief and Rehabilitation Administration
IYC	International Year of the Child
CEDC	Children in Especially Difficult Circumstances
ORS	Oral Rehydration Salts

Index

D

P

Q

R